D0501559

Drew, Elizabeth.
Citizen McCain

ALSO BY ELIZABETH DREW

ELIZABETH DREW

CITIZEN McCAIN

SIMON & SCHUSTER

New York London Toronto Sydney Singapore

SIMON & SCHUSTER
Rockefeller Center
1230 Avenue of the Americas
New York, NY 10020

Copyright © 2002 by Elizabeth Drew
All rights reserved,
including the right of reproduction
in whole or in part in any form.

SIMON & SCHUSTER and colophon are registered trademarks
of Simon & Schuster, Inc.

For information regarding special discounts for bulk purchases,
please contact Simon & Schuster Special Sales at
1-800-456-6798 or business@simonandschuster.com

Designed by Ellen Sasahara

Manufactured in the United States of America

1   3   5   7   9   10   8   6   4   2

Library of Congress Cataloging-in-Publication Data
is available.

ISBN 0-7432-3002-7

For David

CITIZEN McCAIN

Chapter 1

"If we have the votes and the guts, we'll prevail."

IN EARLY JANUARY 2001, at breakfast in the Senate Dining Room, John McCain was in an upbeat mood. The large, ornate room was nearly empty; the new Congress had only recently convened and the new President wasn't to be sworn in for another couple of weeks.

McCain was already revved up for the next round in the battle he had been waging for many years to reform the nation's campaign finance laws. For McCain, campaign finance reform was about a broader ethic. As he demonstrated in his campaign for the Republican nomination in 2000, he sees it as essential to restoring the public's faith in politics, and also to attracting young people into politics and government service. For him, it has much to do with the very definition of the country, the workability of the democratic idea.

In the coming year, McCain was to broaden his agenda, become arguably the most interesting figure in American politics—nearly as popular and at times more popular than even the President—and point the way toward a new kind of reform politics. And in the weeks after the terrible events of September 11, his was the most consistently sought-after, and the clearest, voice out of Washington. During this time, he defined the situation, rallied the public's morale, and soothed it when it became fearful.

He understood that there was a more civic-minded streak, an idealism, in the public than more conventional politicians appealed to. His disdain for the conventions of politics had gained him a large following—which went beyond the more than six million people who voted for him in 2000. He had an effortless feel for the national psyche and a natural instinct for the right thing to say. His efforts in the course of the year were to reveal new aspects of his character.

Now, as he undertook his seventh year of leading the effort to reform the campaign finance system, there were reasons for optimism. The Democrats had picked up four Senate seats in the previous election, the new Democratic senators providing a presumed four more votes for reform, and the Senate was now divided 50–50, with the Republicans in nominal control because vice-president-elect Dick Cheney could break a tie. (This was before James Jeffords switched from being a Republican to being an Independent.)

McCain's effort to enact reform of the campaign finance system had met with defeat in the Senate five times in the past six years. The House passed its version of his bill twice by wide margins, so the Senate became the crucible. A majority of the Senate had supported McCain's bill in the past—or ostensibly so—but the opponents of change, led by Republican Senator Mitch McConnell, of Kentucky, and Majority Leader Trent Lott, first choked off debate so that amendments couldn't be offered to broaden support and then killed the bill by filibuster. Now McCain was determined to have an open debate, which could help him attract additional support by accepting amendments sponsored by senators who were on the fence. It would also help prevent Democrats who didn't want reform but didn't want to say so from playing devious parliamentary games, and hiding behind McConnell, as they had in 1999.

Referring to the last time he had fought for his bill, in 1999, when some of his Senate colleagues ripped into him because he had accurately called the current system corrupt, McCain said, "I'm not going to let them pull me into a personal combat. That was my worst test. I'm not going to engage in that again." McCain was in fact to make an important strategic change based on that lesson.

At the same time, McCain believed that the current campaign finance system was more of a plague on the body politic than ever. He said, "It's badly skewed our priorities, and blocked badly needed legislation to help the American people. It's never been worse in my time here. It affects everything: the tax code, the military, Medicare, Social Security, gambling—you name it. I can give you a list of twenty issues that haven't been acted on, or cite the Telecommunications Act of 1996, which was nothing like reform." Of that bill, McCain often said, "All the interests were at the table but the public interest."

"I'm just going to go ahead," McCain said over the breakfast in early January. "It's obvious that the longer you wait, the harder it is. On January 22, or whatever day we start business, I'll ask unanimous consent to move to consider our bill. If they block it, I'll come back the next day and the next day and then we'll have to start tying things up—and they have to know that. We just won't let them proceed. The first bill they bring up, we'll offer it as an amendment. They don't have sixty votes for cloture now [the number needed to shut down a filibuster] or even fifty-one votes to block us by tabling my amendment."

Tom Daschle, the Senate Democratic leader, had already told McCain that the Democrats would stick with him at least on the early procedural issues. McCain said, "All it boils down to is if we have the votes and the guts, we'll prevail."

McCain's presidential campaign struck a chord when he told

people he would "shake things up in Washington." Public disgust with the role of money in our political system was rising, and he gave it voice. The amount of money spent in a presidential election had grown by more than half a billion dollars since 1996, to $2.75 billion in the 2000 election. The amounts in themselves, though quite large, were less significant than what they reflected: the ever-increasing time that the politicians had to spend raising the money, the access and commitments (spoken or understood) that came with accepting that money, especially the six- or seven-figure amounts in "soft money"—unregulated union, corporate, or individual contributions.

Another factor in McCain's favor now was that senators who had recently been through a campaign, or were about to undergo one, were becoming increasingly alarmed at both the amounts of money they had to raise and the number of ads by outside groups, some of mysterious origin, that could come at them from any direction.

A small band of Republicans had been with McCain in previous fights, but he needed some more in order to head off a filibuster against his bill. Despite his optimism McCain knew that he was asking incumbents to do a very hard thing: to change the system by which they'd been elected. He said, "This threatens every lobbyist on K Street. This threatens every business interest. So you can't underestimate the opposition. This thing will be trickier and more devious than anything I've ever done. It's a house of mirrors."

President-elect George W. Bush had shown scant interest in reform. After McCain walloped him in New Hampshire, Bush's aides redesigned their candidate as "a reformer with results" for the next contest, in South Carolina, and Bush offered a campaign finance proposal that wasn't taken very seriously and that Bush himself made little of during the rest of the campaign.

Since the election, the two men had had only perfunctory contact—though McCain had campaigned with Bush in five states. McCain had also campaigned for about forty Republican House candidates and was credited by Tom Davis, the chairman of the House Republican campaign committee, with keeping the House in Republican hands. "I made a mistake early on," McCain said. "Several months before the election, I campaigned for a couple of guys who weren't for campaign finance reform. The opponents who were Democrats and were for campaign finance reform wrote me and said, 'What's the deal here?' I thought their complaints were legitimate, so after that I only campaigned for people who were for campaign finance reform. That's why I didn't go to the State of Washington for Slade Gorton [an incumbent Republican senator who lost narrowly] and didn't go to a number of places. If they weren't for it, I didn't go. Some changed their positions."

The McCain-Bush nomination struggle had left a substantial residue of bitterness between both the two men and their respective staffs. The McCain people remained especially bitter over the rough tactics that the Bush campaign and its allies had employed in South Carolina. The onslaught against McCain involved not just attacking his character but also distorting his campaign positions and spreading ugly rumors about his family. A retired Democratic South Carolina politician described it later as "the dirtiest, nastiest campaign I've ever seen." Mark Salter, McCain's closest aide, said, "I can't for the life of me see why *they* have a grudge against *us*." The Bush camp's resentment obviously stemmed from the fact that McCain had interrupted what was supposed to be Bush's stately march to the Republican Party's coronation. McCain defeated Bush in eight primaries, and though he made some missteps of his own, he was ultimately defeated by Bush's superior resources and closed primaries in which only Republicans could vote. (McCain had been winning among Independents and had succeeded in pulling new people, especially young people, into politics.) When President-elect Bush first came to

Washington in December to confer with congressional leaders, he referred to McCain distantly as "my former opponent."

A few days after the election, Bush called McCain, and McCain suggested that they needed to meet and talk about campaign finance reform. Bush agreed. Later, Bush called McCain to thank him for holding an early hearing on his proposed Commerce Secretary but didn't bring up the issue of reform. "He didn't bring it up, and I didn't bring it up," McCain said. "Look, whenever he and I have a conversation, it's always cordial."

But McCain believed that Karl Rove, Bush's chief political strategist during the election, was controlling the political agenda. Much of the bitterness between the two campaigns got back to Rove, who was not only Bush's chief political tactician but also had a longstanding feud, going back to their early days as consultants, with McCain's political director, John Weaver. Though McCain had made it clear the previous summer that he would have waged the campaign finance fight whether Bush or Gore had won the Presidency ("We will have blood all over the floor of the Senate"), McCain said on that early January morning, "Don't underestimate the anger that this has generated among people like Karl Rove. 'Here's that spoiler McCain again.' I'm really intent on keeping smiling, no matter what they do, keep the game face on"—a typical McCain expression.

McCain wanted early consideration of his bill because procedural delays could work against getting it through the Congress at all. And he had his eye on Bush's pen. McCain said, "It just seems to me that if we pass a bill early on by pretty significant margins, he'll have to think long and hard before vetoing it." In fact, McCain and his aides suspected that, with the help of Majority Leader Lott, the White House was pursuing a veto strategy: The later the bill got through Congress—if it did—the easier it would be for Bush to veto it because he would have other victories under his belt. McCain was already trying to collect enough commitments to show that this time he would have sixty votes to shut off a filibuster.

Meanwhile, Mark Buse, McCain's aide for campaign finance reform legislation, had already begun negotiating with a Lott aide about when the bill could be brought up. Lott offered to let that happen after Congress finished work on all of the appropriations bills, which usually means the end of the year. "I told Mark," McCain said, " 'Tell him we were entertained by their offer.' " "Entertain" is another McCain word, often used sarcastically. Though McCain is dead serious about the issues he takes on, he doesn't take the give-and-take, the legislative gamesmanship, too solemnly. There's a streak of the mischievous in him, the scamp, which adds to his enjoyment of what he does and helps him get through the day. This streak also helped him survive the North Vietnamese prison camps. His highest form of praise for someone is to tell them, "We'd have had fun in the camps."

Despite his threats, McCain was actually angling for the bill to be brought up in March. He had more public support to build, more allies to acquire. But he was thinking ahead.

McCain's view of human relations seems to be heavily influenced by his five-and-a-half years in "the camps" in North Vietnam: He and his allies would never betray each other. And that's how, at the beginning of the year, he viewed his close friend Chuck Hagel, of Nebraska, one of four senators who had backed McCain's presidential campaign. Unbeknownst to McCain, Hagel was already talking to the White House about his own proposal. While McCain would completely abolish soft money, Hagel would enshrine it in national law for the first time by capping soft money contributions at $60,000 per year—but also leaving a gaping loophole. Mitch

McConnell, the archfoe of campaign finance reform, was talking up Hagel's proposal in the Senate Republican Conference; it also had the support of Republican strategists and lobbyists. It gave reform opponents something to be for.

"We are as close as you can be in the Senate," McCain said of Hagel, "but that doesn't bridge our disagreement on some issues. I know he would not do anything to harm me. I think all he wants is a vote on his proposal. Maybe Mitch may throw votes behind him, but I don't think he has fifty-one. We'll fight it out, and if there's a glaring loophole that emasculates campaign finance reform, I'll vote against final passage and be done with it."

Chapter 2

"I don't know who's driving the train."

ON THE MORNING of January 22, the Monday after Bush's Inauguration, McCain and his co-sponsors hold a press conference in the Senate radio-television gallery, on the third floor of the Senate side of the Capitol, to announce their bill, which McCain will shortly introduce on the Senate floor. (The Inaugural weekend had been an orgy of access-selling, with especially generous donors given entrée to special parties with the powerful or prime seats in the stands along the parade route.)

In order to press his claim for an early and open debate on his bill, McCain has been making a number of television appearances—he's a popular guest on the talk shows because he can be counted on to say something provocative—to keep the pressure on the administration to make a deal to bring up the bill before too long. He's also been working to line up enough supporters to show that he could get sufficient votes to cut off a filibuster.

When it was suggested by interviewers, or by Republicans, that he was trying to get in the way of Bush's program by pushing campaign finance reform first, McCain would point out that there was no Bush legislation ready to go before the Senate. Administration bills would first have to be drafted and then considered by congressional committees before they could be brought to the Senate floor. "I'm not interested in interfering with President Bush's agenda," McCain would say.

Mark Buse and Lott's staff continued to negotiate over when the campaign finance bill might be brought up, and McCain met with Lott in Lott's office. Lott offered to let the bill come up in May, with no filibuster and no tricks to prevent amendments that might broaden support for the bill. Lott told McCain, "Look, I'll just tell you I think the President ought to be able to move his agenda first."

McCain replied, "I don't disagree, if it was ready. But we all know, history tells us, that it's not ready. And once he sends it it has to go to committee first, and that's going to take time. There's nothing else legislatively to do, so let us go." McCain said that he would like the bill to come up in mid-March and be completed by the Easter recess. This had actually been his goal all along, but he felt that he had to keep the pressure on, which turned out to be correct. Lott told him he'd get back to him.

Standing with McCain at the press conference to introduce his bill are his key Democratic co-sponsor, Russ Feingold, of Minnesota, and Carl Levin, Democrat of Michigan and a strong supporter of reform. Also there are some of the handful of Republicans who have stood with him before: Susan Collins and Olympia Snowe, both of Maine; Jeffords; and Fred Thompson, of Tennessee. They've been joined by McCain's latest, and important, catch: Thad Cochran, a mainstream conservative from Mississippi. Cochran, with his white-thatched hair, stereotypical of what we used to think senators looked like, is a gentle and immensely civilized man, none too close to his more rough-hewn and partisan fellow-Mississippian, Trent Lott. Cochran is a respected senior figure in the Senate and closer to what McCain calls "the old bulls" than any of the other supporters of the bill. He is up for reelection in 2002, and in the course of the 2000 election, he became disturbed by the ever-increasing amounts of money that had to be raised and the plethora of ads that could come into the race from outside groups—for or against a candidate.

One day late last year, Cochran took McCain aside at a Senate Republican policy lunch and told him that he would support his bill. This gave McCain eight Republicans of whose support he could be certain. Also at the press conference are Martin Meehan, Democratic congressman from Massachusetts, and Christopher Shays, an intense Republican congressman from Connecticut. Shays and Meehan had co-sponsored the House counterpart to the McCain-Feingold bill and had been involved in the discussions about what this year's bill should contain. The House and Senate sponsors had worked together in the past but this year were to be thrown into an even closer partnership. The idea from the outset was to try to get a bill through the Senate, which had traditionally been the burial ground for the legislation, that the House would also accept. The purpose was to avoid a House-Senate conference that could give the bill's opponents an opportunity to kill it there by tying it up in lengthy negotiations.

Though Feingold's name has been on the campaign reform bills along with McCain's, the two men, while utterly cordial, aren't close friends. But when McCain went shopping some years ago for a Democrat to co-sponsor his bill, Feingold was the only one who was willing to join him, and McCain respects and is grateful to him for that.

Feingold, a serious man, comes from a long tradition of Wisconsin reformers. In the 1998 election, he refused to accept soft-money ads from his party (some ran anyway, as did soft-money ads from outside groups) and won only narrowly. As a purist, he's a bit of a loner in his party caucus, so for intelligence about what was going on among the Democrats, McCain and his staff rely on Carl Levin, a very brainy man, and Chuck Schumer, of New York, who was to become increasingly involved in the reform effort. Throughout the many struggles over the McCain-Feingold bill, Feingold's opinion had to be taken into account, but there was no doubt in anybody's mind that McCain was the senior partner, the major strategist, the star.

Fred Thompson, the hulking former Watergate attorney and movie actor, one of the four senators who backed McCain in 2000 and one of his closest friends, jokingly complains that McCain is now calling the bill "McCain-Feingold-Cochran." "I think I was the third person to sign onto this bill. Now that it's achieved such popularity, John, I'd like my name mentioned more often."

McCain laughs, "It will be referred to as 'the Thompson bill' from now on." McCain is partial to people who make him laugh, and Thompson is one of the funniest men in the Senate.

In its latest version, the bill banned soft money and also barred labor unions and corporations from using their treasury money (soft money) to run electioneering ads for or against a candidate (which they pretend are "issue ads") within sixty days of an election, thirty days of a primary. These groups wouldn't be barred from running such ads, just from paying for them with soft money, on the grounds that such contributions to federal elections had long been barred by law.

In fact, corporate funds had been banned from federal campaigns during the Theodore Roosevelt administration, in 1907, and union dues by the 1947 Taft-Hartley law. Individual contributions had been strictly limited by the post-Watergate Federal Election Campaign Act of 1974, the broadest campaign reform law to date. But they all had crept into federal elections, as soft money, through a loophole created at the parties' behest by the Federal Election Commission in 1978. The idea was that such money would be used for nice, benign, "party-building activities," such as get-out-the-vote drives. But it had evolved into something else entirely. The 1974 Act worked well enough for the 1976 election—probably the cleanest one in a long time—and then the soft money loophole began to erode it, and now it has been largely destroyed. In effect, the parties act as laundries for money that isn't supposed to be used in federal elections. A fat soft-money donation to the party will gain the donor access to congressional leaders and a seat at the table when decisions are made on legislation. It'll get the attention of a President.

In the 2000 election, nearly half a billion dollars was raised in soft money, almost twice the amount that was raised in 1996; most of it was used for ads on behalf of a candidate, which were questionable because they were paid for with money that is ostensibly illegal in federal campaigns.

McCain's most recent bill had left out the ban on using soft money for electioneering ads because opponents had made too much trouble over its alleged unconstitutionality—often using bogus, if somewhat effective, arguments. But the large increase in the number of ads in 2000 caused numerous senators to ask him to put the provision in his new bill. Also, a number of senators had expressed a concern that if the parties were barred from using soft money, it would simply flow over into electioneering ads by outside groups. Bona fide issue ads—such as the famous "Harry and Louise" ads against the Clintons' mammoth health-care plan—were not touched by this provision. And other advocacy groups were still allowed to run electioneering ads, as long as the contributions for them were disclosed.

McCain wanted the limit on contributions by individuals, set at one thousand dollars in the 1974 campaign finance reform act, to be raised to two thousand dollars as partial compensation for banning soft money, which was making its way into individual candidates' campaigns, and also to partially compensate for the amount that the one thousand dollars would be in current terms (about three thousand dollars), after inflation. But Feingold was resistant to raising the amount, and so the bill left it alone—though Feingold did indicate privately that if all else went well enough, he might be amenable to raising the thousand-dollar limit.

Introducing his bill at the press conference, McCain said, "The evidence is clear that we should have taken it up today. But we want to cooperate."

McCain was trying to not appear to be getting in the way of the White House, to simply be causing trouble for Bush out of spite. He didn't want to be seen as George Bush's Bobby Kennedy; he needed to depersonalize the fight. So did the President. So, on Saturday, January 13, Bush called McCain in Arizona and suggested that they should get together. McCain told Bush, "This isn't a rivalry between us but I have to do this and we have to work it out."

Bush said that he understood, and wanted to work with him on it, but no serious collaboration between the two men on this issue was to come about. Nevertheless, shortly before the Inauguration, a Bush aide announced that the President would meet with McCain on Wednesday, January 24. The first time McCain learned of the meeting was when he read about it in the papers that Friday. And as of the next Monday morning, his office still hadn't heard anything from the White House. Asked about this by reporters at the press conference, McCain pretended to be holding onto the bars of the White House gate and said, impishly, "Maybe I should be at the gates first thing in the morning."

•   •   •

Only a few people were on the Senate floor when McCain entered to introduce his bill, and he spoke briefly. This was largely a ceremonial task. Normally, oratory wasn't his forte. His talents and ability to persuade lay elsewhere: in the way he made the case, in his persona, his moral authority. On the Senate floor he said, "We must overcome the cynicism that is growing rampant in our society." He added, "After one of the closest elections in our nation's history, there's one thing the American people are unanimous about—they want their government back. We can do that by ridding politics of large, unregulated contributions." Closing, he said, "I believe we see a light at the end of the tunnel—which is an old line from the Vietnam War." And then, unable to remain somber for too long, he said, "When a soldier in Vietnam was told that, he said, 'Yeah, the light at the end of the tunnel is a train.' " He added that he hoped that wouldn't be the outcome in this case.

McCain was planning a town meeting in Arkansas on Monday, and after he came off the Senate floor, he instructed Buse to make sure that Feingold could get there. Then he said, "Lott has to get fifty-one votes to bring up another bill first, and he can't get fifty-one votes. The Democrats have to vote with me. Fred Thompson will never abandon me. Susan Collins will never abandon me. So what are they going to do?"

As McCain got aboard the subway to go back to his office in the Russell Building, a tourist came along and said, "Senator, I support your position on campaign finance reform." McCain was getting used to being stopped by tourists on Capitol Hill now. He was a different personage than he was before the 2000 campaign. And he knew it, and he was using it.

The meeting between Bush and McCain at the White House was for the purpose of what Washington calls "optics." Bush would be seen as wanting to work with McCain. An adviser to the White House said, "It's better to have this be about issues than about personalities." McCain was well aware that he was being used by the White House, but he needed to be seen as cooperative as well.

To McCain's surprise, the meeting, which began at 5:00 P.M. and lasted forty-five minutes, was held in the Oval Office rather than in the private residence, as he had been led to expect. Another surprise was that Vice-President Cheney was also at the meeting. Some Republican allies of McCain's had tried to persuade Cheney to urge the White House to cooperate with McCain, but Cheney had made it clear that he was against reform, telling some people that he thought it would hurt the Republican Party (which had an advantage in fund-raising). After some chit-chat about issues they had in common—reforming the military, fighting "pork-barrel" spending (a longtime hobby horse of McCain's)—Bush and McCain got to the subject of campaign finance reform. From time to time, Cheney expressed misgivings about reform. He said that previous reform laws hadn't worked, which wasn't totally the case. The meeting was polite enough. McCain explained the provisions in his bill, and Bush said that he went along with the idea of abolishing soft-money contributions by labor and corporations, but not by individuals. (That was his position in South Carolina.) This would of course leave a large loophole in the law, allowing an individual donor to contribute millions.

McCain tried to explain to Bush why a provision Bush favored, called "paycheck protection," which would require that unions get the prior approval of members before spending their dues on political activities, wasn't necessary, since in McCain's bill, union activities would be curbed in other ways. Paycheck protection was a classic "poison pill" that Republicans had used in the past to try to defeat reform bills; if it was adopted, Democrats could be counted on to vote against the bill. But it was of questionable effectiveness because it had been defeated in the past by fairly large margins. McCain well understood that "paycheck" was unlikely to be adopted by the Senate; all Senate Democrats, plus his Republican allies, and perhaps some other Republican senators in states with a strong labor presence, would vote against it. But he was trying to persuade Bush not to use it as a rationale for vetoing the bill. When McCain told Bush that paycheck protection was a "straw man," and a "nonstarter" with the Democrats, Bush didn't reply. (McCain later told his staff that he didn't think that Bush understood the paycheck issue.)

Bush told McCain that House Whip Tom DeLay, a fierce opponent of campaign finance reform, had asked him to promise, in writing, that he would veto McCain's bill, but, Bush said, he had declined to do so. Bush was trying to look reasonable, and so was McCain. When he emerged from the White House, McCain seemed almost robotic when he said such things as, "I believe I come away with the distinct impression that he's favorably disposed toward continued discussions on this issue."

The next morning, in his office, McCain said, "I don't know who's driving the train. I don't know if it's Cheney. Rove? I don't know if their strategy is to veto it or try to bury it here. If I were in their shoes, I'd say, 'Let's sit down with McCain and see if there's any accommodation that can be made.' " But McCain was not to hear directly from the White House on the matter again.

McCain said that if he didn't get an agreement the following week on bringing up the bill in March, he'd go to the floor to try to force the issue. Asked if he thought that the Democrats would like to kill reform legislation, as many observers thought, he replied, "Everybody would like to do that. But the pressure of public opinion will keep them from doing that."

Asked if he'd been in touch with Hagel lately, McCain replied, "I talked to Chuck this morning. We intend to work together. One thing I'm confident of is he's not trying to sandbag me."

•   •   •

Chuck Hagel didn't set out to sandbag McCain when he first offered his proposal in 1999 as a compromise. The story of these two men is the story of how two politicians, highly competitive by nature—and in this case two decent men—can get overtaken by their competition.

Handsome and broad-gauged, also a Vietnam War hero, Hagel was understood to be a finalist on Bush's vice-presidential list (that is, if Bush was actually considering anyone other than Cheney). The vice-presidential brush, as well as his range—Hagel can do foreign policy and economics as well as politics—had made him a familiar figure on television in recent months. But, like McCain, he had an independent streak and hadn't been especially popular with the Senate Republican leaders; they believed he spoke his mind a bit too much in party conferences, and also out of school.

Hagel saw up close what happened to McCain when he ran against the party structure. If Hagel was to run for national office in the future, he'd have to find a different way. More than one close observer of Hagel—people who like him—began to see his pursuit of his own campaign finance proposal as one that would help him "get well" with the establishment of the Republican Party.

The very fact that McCain seemed to have his best chance yet to get a bill marshaled the forces threatened by him. The Washington lawyers who specialize in election law were telling their respective parties' senators that by abolishing soft money, the McCain-Feingold bill would weaken the national parties. Further, they argued, soft money that had gone into the party coffers would now slosh over into even more ads by outside groups. To what extent this would happen, no one knew, but it was a useful argument, giving an ostensibly respectable reason for opposing the ban on soft money, to which both parties had become addicted.

Democrats had other reasons for pause. In 2000, they had essentially caught up with the Republicans in raising soft money, while the Republicans outraised them in "hard," or restricted, contributions. But the Democrats' interest in maintaining parity on soft money could turn out to be shortsighted, since they achieved it when the soft-money king, Bill Clinton, was in the White House. In 2000, Bush raised even more soft money for his Presidential race than Clinton had in 1996, and now he was in the White House, with all its fund-raising advantages.

At the same time, the AFL-CIO, which in the past had taken a fairly relaxed view on reform proposals, since it could be confident they wouldn't become law, became very worked up over the latest version of McCain-Feingold, especially the part prohibiting them from using their treasury money for electioneering ads. This, too, raised the question of how many Democratic senators might abandon reform. McCain and his staff were of the view that there were only a minority of senators in each party who were genuinely for reform. If a bill were to pass the Senate, others would have to be shamed into supporting it. That's why McCain was insistent upon an open process in the Senate. Then he would go to work, bringing pressure from both inside and outside the Senate, putting his formidable flair for public relations to work. Recently, he had helped form an organization called Americans for Reform, a broad coalition of groups including the citizens' lobby Common Cause; the Committee for Economic Development, a group of leading businessmen and economists; the League of Women Voters; the American Heart Association; the Sierra Club; and the group was to sponsor six town hall meetings before the bill was to come to the Senate floor. Each locale was chosen with specific media markets—aimed at specific senators—in mind.

. . .

On Friday, January 26, at another meeting between McCain and Lott, Lott surrendered. "What do you need?" he asked and agreed to grant McCain what he was seeking: two weeks of open debate on the bill in March. There would be three hours of debate on each amendment. McCain wanted this in order to have a real opportunity to study what was in an amendment that the opponents offered, and what it might mean, or to convince allies to oppose or support it. Lott also indicated to McCain that he would oppose a filibuster. Lott was being pragmatic. If McCain didn't quite have sixty sure votes to end a filibuster, he had enough to convince the Republicans that he could get the rest.

And so, through sheer bloody-mindedness, McCain succeeded in getting campaign finance reform on the Senate agenda—when and under the terms that he wanted. No one else could have done it—or would have dared to try.

Chapter 3

"It's most important for me to maintain an atmosphere of nonconfrontation."

McCAIN'S OFFICE, and the way he runs it, are unusual in several respects. Most senators' offices sit at the end of a labyrinth of aides' cubicles, so that upon being seen into the great one's office, one feels that one has been ushered into the sanctum sanctorum. McCain's office, however, sits in the middle of nine parallel rooms that line up on the Russell Building's second-floor hallway. (The former occupant of the suite used a grand office at one end.) The doors to McCain's office are left open unless he's holding a highly sensitive meeting, and aides go freely through it to get from one room to another. His office has an informal atmosphere and is decorated—a term used loosely in this case—with Arizona pictures and books and family photographs. No grand chandeliers or ornate décor. The top of his desk, which a small brass plaque indicates was used by Barry Goldwater (whose Senate seat from Arizona McCain had inherited), has a collection of gewgaws: medals, books, a baseball autographed "To John McCain, a great American" by Ted Williams.

McCain's top aides call him "John," rather than "Senator," as most of his colleagues invite. But the most striking thing about

McCain's aides is how long they've been with him. McCain is known to have a prickly personality at times and a combustible temper, but his aides have been with him for an unusually long time. By 2001, Mark Salter, forty-six, his chief of staff, had been with him for twelve years. Salter was the coauthor of McCain's campaign biography, *Faith of My Fathers,* and knows McCain's mind as well as anyone. Salter, who has a short brown beard and close-set blue eyes, is intense, focused, and speaks quietly. But when he does, McCain listens carefully. McCain often rounds the partition between his office and Salter's, a cramped space next door, and sprawls in the big blue leather chair to talk about all manner of things.

Mark Buse, thirty-five, had been with McCain for an almost unheard of seventeen years, having started as an intern when McCain was in the House and then become staff director of the Senate Commerce Committee, a job that spans a great many subjects from transportation to communications—as well as McCain's main legislative aide on campaign finance reform. Buse, tall and gangly, slightly bald, is noisy and expressive, often waving his arms as he talks.

Nancy Ives, thirty-three, had been McCain's communications director for five years; this may be the most brutal of Capitol Hill jobs. In Ives's case it's a matter of pleasantly and competently fielding the multitude of requests for interviews with McCain, for McCain appearances on television, of answering questions on McCain's position on one thing or another—all of which she does with remarkable calm, even when some stupid question, or the fifteenth question on the same matter, causes her to hold the phone away from her head and roll her eyes. McCain had had only four press secretaries in his nineteen years in the House and the Senate, and in that same period of time only two schedulers (also a high-pressure job). Some senators are well-known on Capitol Hill for their rapid staff turnover, or their nearly brutal treatment of aides.

Despite the relative informality of McCain's office, it's not like summer camp or a commune. Everyone knows who's in charge, a military man to boot. They move briskly at his call and know when he's to be left alone. And when he wants to schmooze, which he does with his staff often. McCain's lack of stuffiness and self-importance carries over into the atmosphere of his office. Politicians present their most pleasant, friendly, backslapping selves to the public and the press. Their relations with their staffs offer a more accurate measure of their character.

McCain can at times become testy for no apparent reason. One senator who admires him says, "Dealing with John is kind of like dancing with a cactus." He does explode on occasion, but he also knows how and when to keep his temper under control. Other senators are known to explode, but McCain's temper is famous in large part because he's famous and in part because he has some dedicated enemies in the Senate. In fact, during the presidential campaign, some of his Senate "colleagues," mainly people in and close to the Republican leadership, conducted a smear campaign suggesting that McCain was unstable. They disliked his independent style and his occasional displays of temper—and they were for George W. Bush. But once they were called on it in a newspaper column, they first denied it and then they stopped it.

There is another aspect of McCain's personality that gets less attention. He may be scratchy at times, but he also has empathy—the empathy of someone who's suffered for someone he sees is hurting. There's a kindness, even a sweetness, that's unusual for people so ordinarily self-centered as politicians.

Washington has a way of reaching a consensus about something, whether or not it's grounded in reality. The consensus spreads through hundreds of conversations, through TV news shows and newspaper columns, and soon enough there's a "wisdom" on some matter or another. Shortly before McCain's bill was to come up in the Senate, the wisdom around Washington was that it was in trouble. Labor was upset. It was widely believed that many Democrats, probably including Senate leader Tom Daschle, wanted to find a way to not back the bill. Several groups opposed to the bill were coalescing around Hagel's proposal, as were Republican Party strategists, including Karl Rove, who through well-placed leaks made it clear that the President was behind it. A Republican strategist said, "Our vulnerable senators up for reelection need to be behind a bill that's not McCain-Feingold. Then they can go home and say, 'I'm for reform.' " That they felt they had to say this was a backhanded testimonial to McCain's new standing.

Just before his bill was to come up, McCain, talking in his office, said, calmly, "We always knew it would have trouble. We're asking incumbents to change the system that keeps them in office. This is a threat to the special interests. It's all going to boil down to this: Are people going to vote against the bill or more likely try to emasculate it and get away with it in the court of American opinion? If they don't think they can, they won't."

McCain and his aides assiduously cultivate that court of opinion: they work closely with influential editorial boards and activist groups. At this point, McCain and his aides believed that though the bill's opponents had said they wouldn't filibuster against its being taken up, there might not be enough votes to stop a filibuster against whatever actual bill emerged. They weren't even sure that whatever bill resulted from the amending process would end up with fifty-one votes.

McCain said, "We knew that the AFL-CIO wouldn't like the bill, so I'm not surprised. The AFL-CIO is working in harness with the Democrats, but that helps us with Republicans. The legitimacy of McConnell's argument that this destroys the Republican Party has been eroded."

It had become Republican dogma that the only reason the Democrats were politically competitive with the Republicans was that they received so much help from labor, including its internal communications with members and its get-out-the-vote drives. (Moreover, the Republican Party in Congress increasingly represented Southern and Southwestern anti-union states.) It followed, according to this dogma, that the only way the Republicans could prevail was by outspending the Democrats. In fact, the Republican Party's allies, in particular the National Rifle Association and the right-to-life groups, had in recent elections mounted effective get-out-the-vote drives. But the mythology dies hard—especially when it's so convenient.

Asked about the fact that John Breaux, a centrist Democrat from Louisiana who had gladly assumed the mantle of power-broker, had just come out against his bill, McCain replied, abruptly, "I'm not surprised by Breaux. Tell me what he stands for."

About Hagel, he said, also abruptly, "We just aren't discussing the issue." He said that this had been the case for a week. Asked what had happened to cause the break, McCain replied, "I became aware that he was pretty well committed to what he was backing. I didn't know that he was working closely with the White House.

"I think he's got it compartmentalized—that he can pursue this and we'll remain friends. He's quoted in the paper as saying he feels like I'm his little brother." McCain's jaw was tight as he said this.

Despite his disappointment, McCain was thinking of inviting Hagel to join a trip to Ireland that he and some other senators were planning to take over the Easter recess. McCain doesn't have many true friends in the Senate—his independent nature, his low tolerance for phonies and his sometimes scratchy personality make many uncomfortable at the least—and he couldn't afford to lose any. Mark Salter said that McCain could compartmentalize, too. But, Salter said, "McCain views this bill as his legacy. He views this as a sacred promise he made to the country."

. . .

Chuck Hagel had direct and indirect encouragement from President Bush to pursue his bill. He'd met several times with Rove and other White House aides, and it had become clear that Rove was driving the train. Hagel had become defensive about his proposal's being called a "stalking horse" for opponents of the bill. Talking just off the Senate floor, he said, "That doesn't bother me because that's not why I introduced the bill. I started this with the intent that there was some possible middle ground here. I know what I believe. I know what my motives are. My motive is to get something that has a majority and that President Bush can sign." He said that Breaux had just told him he thought he could find more Democrats to support his bill. "And I'm in very good shape with most of the fifty votes in my caucus."

As big a problem for McCain was how many Democrats would support the bill. They were in fact divided, and the main question was where Daschle, the canny minority leader, would ultimately come out. The Democrats were at that point within one seat of retaking the Senate, and they were being told by the election lawyers and consultants (who benefit handsomely from the current system) that the bill would be to their disadvantage. Daschle had been sounding as if he was all for McCain's bill. Most Democrats in fact were saying that they were for the bill, but, with a few exceptions, it was impossible to tell where they really stood. Probably no other issue elicits more double-talk and evasion: "I'm for the bill, but only if it's real reform," etc. Some Democrats were said to be following a "veto strategy"—they'd help pass McCain-Feingold and hope that Bush vetoed it. For them, that would be the best of all worlds. One Democratic senator, asked about the mood in his caucus, replied, "Terror. Horror. 'How did we get here?' Several in the caucus have said we need soft money."

Various Democratic senators said that if there were a secret ballot, the McCain-Feingold bill would receive only about twenty-five to thirty Democratic votes—not enough to pass it. But the voting in the Senate wouldn't be by secret ballot, of course, and that was where McCain's potential strength lay. That, plus his standing. A Democratic senator who didn't want to be named remarked, "Most Democrats have an investment in McCain-Feingold—not an emotional investment, but they've spoken for it and called for it in the past, when the Republicans were killing it. So they're nervous but in most cases are resigned to supporting it. Unless they can say 'This is no longer McCain-Feingold.' They've made a pledge to the folks back home. This has taken on a life that's larger than the legislation because of McCain's presidential campaign. He has a credibility that most other members don't have on an issue. He's created a constituency for reform. So when my colleagues go home they'll have to do a lot of explaining if they vote against him."

On the Friday before the Monday the bill was to come up, McCain was pleased that so far no other Democrats had followed Breaux in supporting Hagel's bill.

McCain had been talking to senators who hadn't yet supported his bill, trying to find ways to get them "invested" in the process of getting it through the Senate. He'd decided to begin on Monday with a "millionaires amendment," which would aid candidates confronted with an opponent willing to spend millions of their own dollars to get elected. This wasn't a new phenomenon, but the election of Jon Corzine in 2000 to a New Jersey seat after he spent $62 million of his own money sent a wave of panic through much of the Senate. (Two other new Democratic senators also won by spending large sums of their own money.)

A millionaires amendment, McCain said, would be one good way to expand support for the bill in the Senate. "It helps. It shores people up and might bring some others aboard because everyone is shocked by the Corzine experience. Millionaires can't vote against it.

"That'll take care of the first day, but there'll be a lot of surprises before this is over, I'm sure. I think our chances are slightly better because it's being reported that we will act this time. Psychologically, that makes people believe that something will be passed, and that modifies their tactics. Not that McConnell isn't still opposed but his tactics have changed: water down, do 'poison pills' as opposed to out-right killing the bill.

"It's most important for me to maintain an atmosphere of non-confrontation—so that we can come together and work something out," McCain said. Then, in a bit of self-mockery, McCain said, "I hope to avoid confrontation for at least a day or two."

Chapter 4

"Like anything else you go through,
you just keep a steady strain."

O N MONDAY MORNING, March 19, the day the debate on his
bill is to begin, McCain is meeting in his office with top aides
Mark Salter and Mark Buse. Also in this morning's meeting is John
Weaver, the political director of the 2000 campaign and then political director of McCain's Political Action Committee, Straight Talk
America. McCain is sitting in a leather chair in front of his desk, one
foot propped on a coffee table. He seems utterly calm.

Salter is worried that the McCain forces don't yet have a plan for
the debate that's to begin on the Senate floor in a couple of hours.
"You wanted a wide open debate," Buse responds, "and you've
got it."

The problem is that McConnell, who as chairman of the Senate
Rules and Administration Committee, is managing the debate for the
opponents of McCain-Feingold, won't divulge what amendments he
plans to bring up, or when. And the time for the forces in favor of
the bill will be controlled not by McCain but by Christopher Dodd,
of Connecticut, the ranking member of the committee. If McCain
wants a certain amendment offered, he has to negotiate with Dodd

and other Democrats. The reform forces aren't sure that Dodd, a former chairman of the Democratic National Committee, is actually in favor of the bill. So McCain isn't really in control of anything—except the strategy for trying to steer the bill through the Senate, and even there he has to reach a consensus among the other supporters.

McCain raises the question with his aides of how to respond to the charge, made by both Democrats and Republicans, that his ban on soft money would weaken the parties. Buse has been discussing with aides to other reform proponents ways of lessening the impact of the soft-money ban so as to gain more support for the bill—without giving Democrats an excuse for abandoning it.

McCain suggests that they discuss the matter in a meeting of reform proponents. He's approaching this debate in an entirely new way. Rather than go to the Senate floor with one or two allies and do battle with McConnell and his allies, he has formed a coalition of twelve Democrats and Republicans, the "principals," who are strongly behind the bill and who will meet each morning or evening in the President's Room, a ceremonial office near the Senate floor, to decide strategy. Unlike past debates on the issue, this was going to be a collective effort.

McCain had told his aides, "We have to make sure other people are in this fight so it's not just me and Feingold out there flailing away," and then he went out and corralled other people to help in his effort. He has asked that the other senators share the burden of carrying the debate on the floor and fighting off hostile amendments. He doesn't want to be out there constantly opposing his fellow Republicans. He doesn't want to be in the position of McCain against his party; he also doesn't want to antagonize Republicans who haven't supported reform before but who might come over to his side. It's not that he minds taking on his party—as his past and future actions would show—but he's being pragmatic, and shrewd, as to what's the best strategy for winning Senate approval of his bill.

Salter suggests that McConnell might first bring up an amendment on "nonseverability." The unfortunate term nonseverability means that if any section of a bill is held to be unconstitutional, the entire law is struck down. By far, most bills have a "severability" clause, as does the pending McCain-Feingold bill. A new campaign finance law would inevitably be challenged in the courts, and amendments might be added that could make it vulnerable. McConnell had been talking up nonseverability in party caucuses, and, to his delight, but not accidentally, a set of "principles" which Bush had put forward a few days earlier called for nonseverability. Bush's principles, a document overseen by Rove, who was aided by Republican Party lawyers, also included "paycheck protection." This was Rove's way of keeping Bush in the debate, but it wasn't serious; as in the campaign, Bush didn't pursue the matter.

McCain says to his aides, "Mitch wouldn't want to bring up 'paycheck' now because he knows he cannot win that."

McCain hopes that the reformers will begin with a millionaires amendment, by Mike DeWine, Republican of Ohio. DeWine was also one of the four senators who supported McCain in 2000, but now he's a co-sponsor of Hagel's bill. McCain hopes to bring him around in the end. Buse says, "I don't think DeWine's ready yet."

McCain replies, "We want Mike to be ready. We've got to talk to Mike."

McCain ducks out to confer with Hagel, whose office is only a few doors down the hall.

Like any good politician, McCain likes to begin a discussion with another pol with easy chit-chat—especially if it's about to turn to a difficult matter. So meeting with Hagel, in Hagel's office, McCain begins by discussing the pending trip to Ireland (which is now in question because of the spreading foot-and-mouth disease), but McCain's real purpose is to urge Hagel to bring up his alternative early. Once Hagel's amendment is defeated, as McCain expects it to be, the real dealing can begin. McCain realizes that some matters, in particular the issue of raising the limits on hard-money contributions, are going to have to be settled by tough bargaining behind closed doors. Also, though he doesn't think Hagel has fifty-one votes for his amendment, he doesn't want Hagel to have time to cut deals to gather more support. McCain suggests to Hagel that their staffs start talking about areas of agreement. He tells Hagel that he and others are interested in working on something to strengthen the parties. (Though McCain couldn't know it at the time, this attempt to meet others' concerns was to cause serious headaches later on.)

McCain says when he returns to his office, "This whole thing's fraught with danger, but we'll see how it's going after the first few days." He wants to talk to some Democrats to see what the impact of labor's unhappiness has been. In the hour remaining before the start of the debate on the bill, McCain, jacket off, scans the political newsletter "Hotline"—he loves political gossip—quickly downs a sub sandwich, and chats.

McCain thinks the Democrats have decided that the bill would put them at a disadvantage, while the current system helps incumbents. "That's another reason for them to try to beat it. The majority of the money goes to incumbents." (In fact, in 2000, ninety-eight percent of House incumbents were reelected, and they enjoyed a more than four-to-one financial advantage over their challengers; twenty-three of twenty-eight Senate incumbents were reelected, and they raised more than twice as much money as their opponents.)

Asked if he's nervous, McCain replies, "I'm fine. Like anything else you go through, you just keep a steady strain." He explains that that's an old Navy saying when ships come alongside each other and the crews throw each other lines.

At five minutes to one, when the debate on campaign finance reform is about to begin, McCain dons his jacket and says to Buse, "Let's go." Speech in hand, he walks down the corridor, takes an elevator down one flight, and gets on the subway to the Capitol. Along the way, tourists, who seem to know what is about to happen, wish him luck.

McCain's opening statement, written by Salter over the weekend, is surprising in several respects—but McCain, the unconventional politician, often surprises. Early on, he thanks McConnell, "our steadfast and all-too-capable opponent, who honestly and bravely defends his beliefs, for agreeing to the terms of this debate." He also thanks the President "for his oft-stated willingness to seek a fair resolution of our differences on this issue. . . . Too often, as this debate approached, our differences on this issue have been viewed as an extension of our former rivalry. I regret that very much." And he also singles out Hagel, "my friend yesterday, my friend today, my friend tomorrow." He's trying to—praying that he can—set a civil tone for this debate. "I sincerely hope that our debate, contentious though it will be, will also be free of acrimony and rancor."

Attempting to undercut any personal animus there may be toward him in the Senate and avoid the antagonistic debates of the past, he says, "I thank all my colleagues for their patience, a patience that has been tried by my own numerous faults far too often. As I beg their indulgence again, please accept my assurance that no matter our various differences on this issue, and my own failings in arguing those differences, my purpose is limited solely to enacting those reforms that we believe are necessary to defend the government's public trust and not to seek a personal advantage at any colleague's expense."

He says that he and his co-sponsors seek fair legislation "that helps change the public's widespread belief that politicians have no greater purpose than our own reelection. And to that end, we will respond disproportionately to the needs of those interests that can best finance our ambition, even if those interests conflict with the public interest." He deals with the oft-stated, if not remarkable, insight on the part of opponents of reform and the town cynics that "politicians will always find a way of circumventing campaign finance laws." He says, "Were we to pass this legislation today, I am sure that at some time in the future, hopefully many years from now, we will need to address some new circumvention. So what? So we have to debate this matter again. Is that such a burden on us or our successors that we should simply be indifferent to the abundant evidence of at least the appearance of corruption and to the public's ever-growing alienation from the government of this great nation, problems that this system has engendered?"

McCain was shortly to find out how difficult it would be to steer a bill through the Senate without having any formal role.

Chapter 5

**"If this were an inside-the-Beltway deal,
we'd be dead."**

To McCain's and Buse's surprise, McConnell first calls on Pete Domenici, of New Mexico, to offer an amendment dealing with wealthy candidates who spend large amounts of their own money on a race. In such a case, the limits on contributions to the opponent would be increased. They had hoped to have Mike DeWine offer his own version, which they thought contained fewer problems. McConnell and McCain had different motivations for offering similar proposals. McConnell saw it as a way of splitting off reformers who would object to lifting limits on contributions. Also, the first news stories wouldn't be about an attempt by opponents to kill the bill—which could fail—but about the senators' voting to protect themselves against wealthy opponents, or "incumbent protection." McCain's motivation was to broaden support for his bill in the Senate.

As soon as McCain and Buse, seated together on the Senate floor, saw Domenici's proposal, they felt that it went too far, and McCain told the Senate, "His is a meat-axe approach to a problem that requires a scalpel."

Domenici offers changes in his proposal, and McCain, looking perturbed, says, "I've got to tell the senator from New Mexico that he has made substantial changes to his amendment," adding, "We've got to figure out what all this means. This is legislating on the fly here." He wants a bill, but he also wants to be sure of what it says and that it contains no constitutional problems. McCain offers to negotiate with Domenici that night, to come up with something more acceptable. Meanwhile, McConnell says, the other side can offer an amendment, but Dodd says that his side isn't ready with an amendment. This is messier than McCain had hoped for, even though he's called this process "jump ball."

McCain and Buse go into the Republican cloakroom, a narrow room behind the Senate floor, to try to find out what is in DeWine's proposal and see if they can't work out a new compromise proposal.

For a while, it seems that perhaps McConnell had guessed right. In the debate, both Dodd and Daschle indignantly say that the millionaires amendment moves the bill away from reform, which is ominous. "This isn't reform," Daschle says. "It makes a mockery of reform." Dodd, the fiery Irishman, says, "If you want to basically gut the bill this is the way to do it."

That evening, in the Republican cloakroom, a number of senators, including McCain, and staff members negotiated over the Domenici amendment. The problem was how much more in funds to allow those candidates facing opponents who spent their own fortunes. Finally, McCain ended it by saying, "I think we have an agreement. Let's grasp it while we have it. Let's go home before we protract the agony." And then he went off to meet with Domenici and his staff. He was being the chief negotiator and facilitator.

Part of the difficulty was that any millionaires amendment raised the contentious issue of increasing the limits on hard-money contributions—still kept at one thousand dollars per individual in the bill. McCain and Buse realized that McConnell had succeeded in exposing the fissures among reformers, or putative reformers, over whether to raise the hard-money limits.

The next morning, a new version of the millionaires amendment, co-sponsored by Domenici and DeWine, with the encouragement and blessings of McCain, is offered. It specifies that if an opponent spends more than a certain amount of his or her own money on a campaign, the limits on hard-money contributions would be increased by up to six times. McCain calmly explains it to the Senate, and says that it can be amended later if need be but should be voted on now. "I fully understand that some very strong supporters of our bill feel they have to vote against this amendment," McCain says. "It will not be an anti-reform proposal."

The compromise was agreed to by a vote of 70–30. Fred Thompson and some of the reformers worried about its constitutionality, since it established different donation limits for different individuals.

But McCain felt that Domenici had been treated cavalierly the day before, when Democrats moved successfully to table (kill) his amendment as a show of strength. McCain managed to salvage the situation, but this morning he told the bipartisan, pro-reform principals, meeting in the President's room, "We're all going to have to be much more careful about how we deal with the opposition." McCain was trying to hold the coalition together by discouraging strong-arm tactics by Democratic reformers. And now, he hoped, DeWine and Domenici were invested in the bill.

Each Tuesday, the Democratic and Republican senators meet separately over lunch, and afterward, reporters gather to catch the most interesting ones for quotes, and so now, in the early afternoon, a group has gathered around McCain on the second floor of the Senate side of the Capitol. He's determined not to let the Democrats slip away so easily over the millionaires amendment. Responding to reporters' questions about the amendment, McCain nonchalantly replies, "It's something everybody knew was going to be addressed. It's every incumbent's fear. I don't see how you can oppose it [the bill] just because it does something about millionaires." He also points out that the vote for the amendment was 70–30. He's asserting his role as the definer of what constitutes real reform. It's a critical role, and he knows it—and he appears confident that he can pull it off. He has the credentials to do it.

He's asked what amendments will come up next.

"They don't tell us."

Asked if he knows when Hagel's proposal will come up, he replies, "I'm in constant communication, but I don't get a lot of information." McCain smiles and sometimes seems to dance on his feet, like a lightweight boxer, when he answers questions from the press. And on occasion, as in this case, he can't resist a jab.

Before lunch, McCain had met with AFL-CIO President John Sweeney and a couple of his aides. Of their main complaints, McCain thought they had a point that state parties ought to be able to use soft money for get-out-the-vote drives even if a candidate for federal office's name was on the ballot. (The bill forbade this.) Carl Levin, a strong supporter of reform from the heavily unionized state of Michigan, was already working on this, with McCain's blessing. McCain was trying to defang the unions' opposition and respond to what he thought was a legitimate objection. But he made it clear that he wouldn't roll over for everything the unions wanted. They particularly objected to the portion of the bill that forbade them (along with corporations) from using their treasury money—soft money—for electioneering ads while other outside interest groups weren't covered. McCain wasn't sympathetic. He told Sweeney, "My goal is banning soft money and dealing with independent expenditures so that all the soft money doesn't flow over there. I want to work with you, but we may have to agree to disagree."

On Wednesday, as McCain and Buse had hoped, Dodd called on Democratic Senator Paul Wellstone, one of the most liberal members of the Senate, to offer an amendment to allow the states to impose a public financing system for candidates for federal office. The general view on Capitol Hill is that the public is far from ready for public financing, and McCain was focused on what he could get through the Senate. He was also looking for an opportunity to demonstrate that he wasn't just voting against Republican proposals. In a conversation on the Senate floor, Feingold asked McCain to support the Wellstone amendment in order to make the left happy.

McCain declined, saying, "I've done nothing but upset the right." The amendment was defeated handily.

In a quick conversation in his office on Wednesday afternoon, McCain expressed his frustration at the pace of the debate and his worry that it wouldn't be finished in the allotted two weeks. Lott had made it clear that he was determined that the following week be devoted to the budget. And then would come the two-week Easter recess. The debate had been relatively civil thus far, in large part because McCain wanted to keep it that way—and also to put off the more contentious issues while he built support for the bill. The previous night, one of Lott's aides said to Buse, "Where's the bloodbath?" Buse replied, "We'll get to it."

After expressing his worry about finishing work on the bill within two weeks, McCain remarked, "They know that as long as we have fifty-one votes to stay on the bill we can keep them from going on to the Budget Act."

McConnell had the option of offering the next two amendments, and McCain had no idea what they'd be.

That afternoon, McConnell called on Republican Orrin Hatch, of Utah, to offer paycheck protection. (Most of the amendments offered by the opponents were drafted by McConnell's staff.) The amendment tried, as the President had suggested in his "principles," to cover both unions and corporations but, as McCain had predicted when Bush suggested it, this idea proved impossible to write into law. (Buse had tried to draft a similar amendment years before and gave up.) On the floor, McCain and Buse read Hatch's amendment and quickly concluded that it was unworkable. McCain called the amendment "nonspecific" and "unenforceable," and said he would move to table it. But he left the real combat to Edward M. Kennedy, a steadfast friend of labor, who McCain knew was eager to take Hatch on. Anyway, he didn't want to keep arguing with Republicans. At that morning's meeting of the principals, McCain had said, "We need you to come out and shoot down amendments, so it's not the John McCain Show, it's not McCain versus Bush, McCain versus McConnell." Before turning the floor over to Kennedy, McCain commended Hatch for his valiant—if futile—attempt to establish parity between unions and corporations. This was notable, since the antipathy between Hatch and McCain was understood to be of unusual depth. It was rumored that Hatch got into the 2000 race in order to head off McCain.

Kennedy pointed out that in the previous week, more than 6.7 billion shares were traded in the New York Stock Exchange. Which stockholders would be asked their permission for a corporation's political spending? Since 99.7 percent of corporations don't have stockholders, how are they affected? Though Kennedy, his loud voice booming throughout the chamber, took Hatch's amendment apart, the two men are good friends, and at the end Kennedy went over to Hatch and hugged him. The paycheck proposal was tabled by an overwhelming vote of 69–31, with nineteen Republicans voting against it.

After that, a string of anti-labor amendments offered by the Republicans were defeated.

McCain is peripatetic on the Senate floor, seldom sitting in his seat for long. When he does, Buse is usually by his side, conferring with him. More often, McCain darts around the Senate floor, talking with members, taking their temperature. Sometimes he sits with his friend Thompson, trading jokes. Sometimes McCain goes over to chat with Hagel; it's all very amiable, but purposeful. Often, he'll go off the Senate floor into the Republican senators' cloakroom where he can chat up more members and partake of the Krispy Kreme doughnuts available on a table. Occasionally, McCain repairs to his hideaway, a small, rather nondescript office on the first floor of the Capitol.

On Wednesday and Thursday, on and off the Senate floor, McCain was engaged in working through the issue of what to do about raising the limits on hard-money contributions. (But he did take time out to attend a press conference with Kennedy and John Edwards, Democrat of North Carolina, on the patients' bill of rights, legislation that McCain, in a significant display of independence, had signed onto as a co-sponsor.)

As he scoots around the Senate floor, McCain is sometimes doing business, sometimes shooting the breeze, usually a combination of both. Sometimes when he talks, he stands on the balls of his feet, as if he can't quite hold all that energy down. At one point McCain went into a meeting on the budget to drag Thompson out to go to the floor to deal with an amendment by Republican Arlen Specter, of Pennsylvania, that McCain thought presented constitutional problems. He met with Hagel for about a half-hour in his hideaway.

So as to avoid the constitutional thickets that previous debates had gotten into—to the reformers' public-relations disadvantage—before this year's debate began, McCain had asked both Thompson and Edwards, a first-termer and a former trial lawyer, to bone up on the constitutional issues that McConnell had raised in past debates. But the great constitutional debate never really came to pass this time. McConnell seemed to be something of a spent force. Moreover, he was in a bit of a bind because he was supporting Hagel's bill, which put limits on soft money and therefore undercut his argument that any regulation of spending was unconstitutional. But if McConnell, facing reality, was no longer trying to kill the bill in the Senate, he was setting traps for it further down the line. Something else was involved, having to do with McConnell's position in the Senate. As the head of the Republican Senate campaign committee, he was held partially responsible by several Republican colleagues for the net loss of five Senate seats in the last two elections. He and Lott, whose strategy had been to block action on much legislation, some of it quite popular, were held responsible by numerous Republican senators for their reduced state, to the point where they now had to share power with the Democrats.

The issue of hard-money contributions had been vexing McCain all week because it could divide the supporters of his bill. But it was where McCain had deliberately steered the conversation on the bill, rather than, as Hagel and McConnell would have preferred, discussing the ban on soft money in federal elections. McCain was adamant that that wasn't negotiable. "I'm not going to repeal two laws on the books."

The hard-money issue involved both what individuals could give to candidates and also the aggregate amounts that individuals could give to candidates, parties, and political action committees. If the one-thousand-dollar limit on individual contributions in the 1974 act had been adjusted for inflation, it would now be thirty-three hundred dollars. Raising funds in one-thousand-dollar increments is numbingly time-consuming. (Thus, in the past couple of years some politicians set up their own soft-money accounts, which was questionable.) McCain had thought all along that a ban on soft money would have to be accompanied by an increase in the limits on individual contributions. The problem was that some of the reform groups were adamant about not raising the limits. Though some Democrats were threatening to desert the bill if the hard-money limits were raised, because, they said, Republicans had more wealthy donors than they did, in fact the Republicans had been raising a higher percentage of their money in small donations than the Democrats did. The contributions limit had become a largely symbolic issue.

When McCain went over to Feingold on the Senate floor on Wednesday to talk about the matter, Feingold told McCain that he could go up to two thousand dollars, but no higher.

"But I have some Republicans who won't go any lower than three thousand dollars," McCain replied.

Just before he left the office on Wednesday night, McCain instructed Buse to start thinking about how to work out the problem of the hard-money limits.

On Thursday morning McCain told the principals, "I want everybody to start thinking about what the final bill will look like." On the floor, McCain asked Thompson to continue to hold off offering his amendment to raise the limit to three thousand dollars, because he wasn't ready to deal with it yet. He asked Susan Collins, a good friend of Thompson's, to talk to Thompson about lowering the amount. McCain told Daschle, "I appreciate the way you're address-ing the issue"—he was referring to Daschle's more positive state-ments. "I want to be sure we don't hurt either party." Daschle told McCain that he was reluctant to raise the hard-money limits because his caucus was so divided on it, but that he was willing to go up a lit-tle bit. (Actually, Daschle was ready to go to two thousand dollars.)

In his office on Friday afternoon, after the first week of debate on the bill—the Senate having recessed so that Democratic senators could go on a fund-raising tour—McCain was busy affirming his role as the definer. Earlier, he'd held forth in the Senate press gallery, pro-claiming the week a success but citing the remaining hurdles; he'd given CNN an interview. McCain's approach was to appear opti-mistic but not overconfident. He didn't want his allies to go slack. And McCain is averse to overconfidence.

On his way back to the Capitol, McCain ran into McConnell at the subway.

"Hi, Mitch," McCain said, smiling. "Going back to work." McConnell smiled back.

"See you on Sunday," McCain said. McCain, McConnell, and Hagel were now regulars on the Sunday talk shows. (The media was still making a big thing of the supposed McCain-Hagel "struggle" long after it was clear, or should have been, that Hagel didn't have the votes.) McCain then said, referring to McConnell, "We've had a cor-dial atmosphere, and I think he appreciates that."

Back in his office, McCain gives a radio interview to Jesse Ven-tura; McCain knows that Ventura's following of Independents is cru-cial to his own cause and might in fact be becoming his own following. He frequently appears on *Imus in the Morning*. McCain has figured out how to tap into the popular culture.

"Listen, my friend," McCain, leaning back in his chair, with one foot on top of his desk and smiling broadly, says in the phone interview with Ventura, "I need you, get over here to Washington, we gotta take some of these guys two out of three. What some of these guys need is a body slam." He tells Ventura, continuing to bond with him, "I know you're fighting some tough battles."

"On a serious note, anything I can do for your bill in Washington, I'll do it," Ventura replies.

Then McCain gives interviews to some other radio programs around the country that Ives has lined up.

Now, pacing around the office while munching on a sandwich, he talks to me about where he thinks things stand. "I'm guardedly optimistic," he says. "But if we don't get it done, there'll be more Denise Riches." McCain has made much of the last-minute pardon that outgoing President Clinton gave to the fugitive financier Marc Rich—a pardon surrounded by generous donations by Rich's ex-wife to the Democratic Party and Clinton's planned library in Arkansas.

McCain says, "I don't think they have the votes for Hagel, but it's still a hurdle."

In working on the hard-money issue, he says, "I go around and talk to all these people—Levin, Snowe, Collins, Thompson—all the time. I see them on the floor and I say, 'Hey, how you doin'? What do you think we need to do here?' You need to get balance. Some people think it's too much; some people think it's too little."

He has also made it a point to stay in communication with Daschle. And earlier that day he had struck up a conversation on the floor with Texas Republican Phil Gramm. Gramm and McCain were understood to have a very poor relationship: McCain had been the chairman of Gramm's 1996 race for the Republican nomination, and McCain didn't appreciate it at all when Gramm signed on early to Bush's campaign four years later. Now Gramm has been threatening to filibuster the final bill. So, despite everything, McCain chats him up as well.

He'd also met with Don Nickles, the Republican Whip and never really a friend, who told him that he would support a ban on soft money if the limits on hard money were increased. This was considered big news, but McCain thought that the increase in hard money Nickles wanted was too high. He sensed that Nickles's real purpose was to cause a split among the reformers over the hard-money issue.

Asked if he thinks Daschle wants a bill—Daschle had been quoted during the week saying that the McCain-Feingold bill was "beginning to change its character, and with each change I think you lessen the opportunity for us to keep the Democrats together"—McCain replies that he believes that Daschle wants to clean up the system.

McCain remarks, "Serious negotiations are going on with people who've been involved in this issue for a long time. Chris Dodd is doing a fine job on the floor but he's never been part of the team of supporters that have been meeting. Daschle's the most important guy. He's the leader."

He explains a crucial part of his strategy—his reliance on and encouragement of outside sources of influence to bring pressure on the Senate. "There are observers who will make judgments about what we do. I'm talking about the *Washington Post* and *New York Times* and opinion leaders across this country. If we do something they think is inappropriate, that emasculates the bill, they'll say so. This is not something being done in a smoke-filled room. Chris Dodd and Tom Daschle will be affected by what they do. If this were an inside-the-Beltway deal, we'd be dead."

McCain makes a call to a radio station in Washington state. "What it's done, Dave, is give people with the big money a megaphone and a seat in front of the room and the little guy gets a seat in the back. I'm fighting every interest in town. How are we going to motivate young people to serve if you have to spend a million dollars to win an election?"

Then he has a conference call with about ten editorial boards around the country.

Aware that he is astride a shaky coalition, McCain has been displaying a sophistication about legislative maneuvering and coalition-building that he hadn't been known for before. He explains, "You may have fifty-one votes or sixty votes for the bill to be considered, but you may not have twenty votes to triple the hard-money limits, so you have to keep the coalition together and get as many as you can. If the vote were tomorrow to stay on the bill, we'd probably have seventy votes, but it's different when you get to specific provisions. It varies from issue to issue. It's too fluid right now. The question is whether we can come together and enough people will say, 'I don't like it but I'll go with it.' I don't know who falls off. It's too complicated. We have to convince the American people to convince these people that they can't take a hike on this bill. But if we fail, we'll be back at it. That's one thing I'm sure of."

McCain hates to be stuck in Washington over the weekend; he usually heads out for Arizona, to his ranch in Sedona, about a two-hour drive north from Phoenix, often hosting friends in its guest cabins. When he's in Washington, he lives in an apartment in Northern Virginia; for the last couple of nights, he's hung around the office after the sessions and had McDonald's cheeseburgers with Buse and Salter.

And now, for the second weekend in a row, he's in Washington to appear on the Sunday shows and to spend Fridays and Mondays, when the Senate often doesn't meet, in pursuit of his large purpose. Before he leaves for the afternoon, he calls into his office Joe Donohue, his thirty-two-year-old personal assistant, who first joined McCain as an intern while attending Catholic University in Washington and who now handles the office mail and helps compile McCain's annual list of pork-barrel projects approved by congressional appropriations committees. Donohue is often the pleased object of McCain's affectionate teasing. ("What are you doing here, you punk?") Now McCain wants Donohue to find a new book on the crusades, by James Reston, Jr., he'd been given during the week. He wants to read it over the weekend. (McCain had left it on his Senate desk.)

Chapter 6

"There are people all over K Street trying to figure out amendments that can hurt this bill."

M cCAIN HAD HAD A BAD DAY YESTERDAY. Since it was a Monday, he and his staff had thought it would be a nothing day—many senators were still out of town and no important amendments were supposed to be brought up, and there were to be no votes until late afternoon. Then yesterday evening, the Senate accepted an amendment by Wellstone to also bar nonprofit advocacy groups— such as the Sierra Club, the National Right to Life Committee, and the National Rifle Association—from using soft money for electioneering ads, just as labor and corporations were barred from doing so in the McCain-Feingold bill, which had deliberately left these nonprofit groups out so as to avoid political and constitutional hazards.

This was the first real blow to the bill, and it had come unexpectedly. Some serious backers of the bill worried that the proposal wasn't constitutional, and if the Senate were to add a nonseverability clause, the Wellstone amendment could bring the whole thing down. Moreover, it broadened—or hardened—the constituency against the bill.

McCain and his allies had thought that the amendment would

be fairly easy to defeat. But about an hour before the vote, Buse noticed that certain Democrats who were supposedly for reform were speaking on the amendment's behalf and heard the rumble among other Republican staff members that their side would support it. Realizing what was brewing, he warned McCain, who had just returned to the floor, "I think we're going to lose it." McCain, who had thought the amendment would fail, saw potential trouble for the bill as a whole.

Salter, who had come to the floor, became very upset. This situation was bad enough in itself, but it also aroused unpleasant memories: McCain's bill in 1998 to discourage children from smoking had come unraveled, beginning with a Wellstone amendment to "improve" the bill. They had feared that some well-intentioned amendments would bring the campaign finance bill down. But they watched helplessly as the highly conservative Gramm whipped Republican senators into voting for a *Paul Wellstone* amendment. McCain occasionally walked to the front of the Senate chamber, where the clerks keep a tally of roll calls, to see how it was going, but he realized this was one he'd lose, and that it was serious.

Even McConnell, who for years had affected a principled position against regulating "political speech," voted for it. And so did most of the Democrats, some because of their loyalty to labor (the AFL-CIO had complained that it was covered by the bill's ban on electioneering ads but that the groups covered in the Wellstone amendment were not), some because they'd been warned by the election lawyers (if they needed to be) about being attacked by more ads by outside groups if soft money was banned. Though Daschle voted against the Wellstone amendment, he was now more suspect than ever. He hadn't kept his troops in line.

A grinning McConnell told reporters later, "I thought a bill that was unconstitutional ought to be made a little bit more unconstitutional." He also said that he himself would challenge the new law in court.

As they left the Senate floor, McCain, Salter, and Buse decided that their public line would be that this amendment made the upcoming vote on nonseverability all the more important.

Reporters who realized what had gone on asked McCain afterward if the adoption of the Wellstone amendment hadn't been an attempt to kill the bill.

McCain replied, "If I thought it was constitutional, I'd have voted for it. Nobody said this would be a day at the beach. This raises the stakes on the nonseverability vote."

McCain isn't one for dwelling on defeat when he's in a fight, and so as he and his staff gathered in his office afterward, he told them, "Now nonseverability is *the* key vote." He was obviously disappointed that Democrats who were supposedly for reform had voted for the Wellstone amendment. That Republicans who opposed the bill cynically voted for something that might kill it was more understandable. "We knew there'd be losses. We knew that it would be tough. This isn't so bad. Keep your game face on." Anyway, he said, "Tomorrow we'll beat Hagel."

Now, the next morning, a cold, clear day, McCain is in the reception room off the Senate floor. Hagel's bill is pending. He looks pale.

"Well last night was very entertaining," he says. "To see Phil Gramm whipping the vote and telling people to change their vote. It was kind of sad to see them tell ole Strom to change his vote." (Strom Thurmond, ninety-eight and ailing, had to be brought to the floor on the arm of an escort and seemed only vaguely aware of what was going on. With the Senate divided 50–50, it rarely votes late into the night, because the Republican leaders might need Thurmond's vote, and he may have gone to bed.) "The bad news is that they put a bad amendment on the bill. The good news is that this puts all the attention on nonseverability.

"It's now up to the Democrats," McCain continues. "If the Democrats keep their people in line on nonseverability, we win. If they don't we lose. We can hold eight or ten of ours."

John Weaver and Rick Davis, McCain's campaign manager in 2000, are walking around the reception room, talking urgently into cell phones. All the troops have been called in. To win the nonseverability vote, McCain and his aides have already thrown themselves into their outside game. Last night they worked to influence editorials that appeared today. They've ginned up such supporters of the bill as the thirty-six-million-member AARP and the Sierra Club to contact their own members, and they've alerted McCain's PAC members to contact Democrats on nonseverability. The Common Cause phone banks are at work.

McCain's aides have alerted allies in New Hampshire and suggested that they call the offices of the numerous would-be Democratic nominees in 2004. More Independents and Democrats than Republicans voted for McCain in New Hampshire. McCain will talk by phone to all three television network anchors today. He's appeared on Don Imus's show twice in the past two weeks. Mark Salter says that there are over six million McCain voters out there and that the McCain people are getting in touch with anyone who had ever e-mailed them.

"I just talked to John Kerry," McCain says. "He's with us on nonseverability. We said we're going to demand a whip count—we'll ask Daschle for one. Daschle has never given us a whip count.

"But you've got to just roll with the punches. I always knew there'd be setbacks. Wellstone allows the perfect to be the enemy of the good. It's what happened to us on tobacco.

"Look, we took a hit, and move on. Don't get disturbed, don't get distressed. Keep on moving and get this done."

In the chamber, Hagel, knowing that he doesn't have the votes, divides his bill into three parts in the hope of getting a victory on at least one of them—and therefore of avoiding stories about a humiliating defeat. "This is real reform," Hagel tells the Senate.

McCain moves to table all three parts of the bill. He had told the other principals that he wasn't going to lead the argument against Hagel, though, so he makes a few remarks and lets others do most of the speaking against Hagel's proposal.

"I appreciate the hard work and sincere effort of the Senator from Nebraska," McCain says, speaking from a lectern that has been placed on his desk. He says that there are some parts of Hagel's proposal he could support as a basis for negotiation, but as for the section allowing soft money, "I must oppose it because the soft-money loophole has made a mockery of campaign finance law."

Hagel loses the first vote on tripling hard-money limits, but wins the next one, requiring more frequent and accessible disclosure of campaign spending. When the vote appears close, McCain switches his vote to one in favor of it, and then so does Thad Cochran. They're throwing the vote to deprive Hagel of a narrow victory, making his amendment look like no big deal. Buse had told McCain that the proposal didn't make much difference anyway. Other reformers follow, making it unanimous. During the roll call on the third section—the centerpiece of his proposal—to allow soft money, it quickly becomes clear that some Republicans who hadn't previously supported reform are now voting with McCain to ban soft money. As the roll call proceeds, McCain moves to the front and embraces Hagel. Hagel's soft-money proposal has been soundly defeated, 60–40.

McCain had never thought Hagel had the votes to put soft money into the law, but this is a bigger victory than he'd expected. John Breaux hadn't produced a single new Democratic vote for Hagel. Twelve Republicans, including three who hadn't before supported reform, voted to kill soft money. Thad Cochran, who had had quiet conversations with some of his colleagues, had made it respectable for conservatives to be for ending soft money.

The White House miscalculated in getting the President so closely associated with Hagel's proposal, which never had a chance. (Cheney is reported to have expressed internally some displeasure about this.)

Like a shot, even before the vote is officially over, McCain and Feingold are in the Senate press gallery. "Of course we're happy we won this," McCain says. Referring to his misfortune of the night before on the Wellstone amendment, and also trying not to gloat, he says, "Look, there's ups and downs. We're happy. We were happy Friday and we'll be happy tomorrow." But McCain is superstitious about appearing too optimistic, so he adds, "We believe there are some very tough days ahead."

He's asked if he changed his vote on the disclosure provision because he saw that he couldn't win that one.

"In the interest of straight talk, yes," McCain replies.

And then he's asked how he would characterize the position of someone who says they can't decide on nonseverability until they see what the whole bill looks like (as some Democrats have been doing).

McCain replies, "Waffling."

On Wednesday, McCain was prepared to try to execute a creative strategy that he and Buse had thought up as they left the Senate floor the day before. The idea was to find a way to raise the hard-money limits without giving Democrats an excuse for abandoning the bill. It had taken some persuading on McCain's part to even get to this point. Fred Thompson agreed to lower his goal of three thousand dollars for individual contributions to twenty-five hundred dollars. Thompson's original proposal was perfectly logical, since it was an adjustment for inflation, but he didn't want to undermine his friend McCain. And he told McCain that he was prepared to compromise further in the interest of getting a bill. Dianne Feinstein, Democrat of California, offered a proposal to limit those contributions to two thousand dollars, and her proposed increases in aggregate contributions were lower than Thompson's. Daschle issued a statement that he could "reluctantly" support Feinstein's two thousand dollars, but that "is as far as I can go."

McCain's and Buse's plan was that Thompson's proposal would be put to a tabling vote, which would fail. But lest Thompson's proposal be the only one standing, which might drive away Democrats, McCain would make sure that Feinstein's also be put to, and survive, a vote—and that both proposals get the same amount of votes. Then the negotiations could begin. This was an ingenious strategy and not an easy one to pull off. In order to do so, McCain called Republican supporters of the bill and asked them not to vote to table Feinstein's proposal. Because of the importance of the pending business, McCain cancelled several appointments that day. He was now being trailed by camera crews. *Nightline* wanted to follow him around the next day. At one point, as he returned to his office, descending the escalator to the subway, Ives talked to him in one ear, telling him about media requests and changed appointments, Buse in the other about pending amendments. They both know to talk fast, to get their word in during one of the few breaks in the action. And he took it all in completely calmly. With both the Thompson and Feinstein amendments pending (it took a lot of huddling on the Senate floor to pull this off), a large group, which included Hagel and Nickles, would repair to the Lyndon B. Johnson Room, on the second floor of the Capitol, near the Senate floor, to sit at a large rectangular table and deal.

Just before the meeting, McCain met with Hagel in his office to ask for his help in the negotiations. Now, on his way back to the Capitol, he says that he hopes the negotiators can split the difference. But he adds, "I don't know. I don't know if either side is willing to do that." Asked if he's concerned about Daschle's latest statement, McCain replies, "There's always statements by Senator Daschle."

During the negotiations in the Capitol, McCain let each participant make an opening statement—or blow off steam—and then got down to the dealing. Hagel turned out to be helpful by pointing out that the section of his bill that would have raised the hard-money limits by substantial amounts had received forty-seven votes. This put the Democrats on notice that they would have to budge. Harry Reid, the Democratic Whip, was saying that they wouldn't budge. Nickles was an unexpected help by suggesting, "Why don't we split the difference?" Twice, Democrats had to leave to discuss the matter with Daschle. After two and a half hours of negotiations, a compromise was arrived at: individual contributions would be raised to two thousand dollars, the aggregate amount an individual could give would also be raised, and the new amounts would be indexed for inflation, to avoid the bind the 1974 limits had put the politicians in.

Back in the Senate, Dodd, who had been speaking out against raising the hard-money limits, says he can "reluctantly" support the agreement. Mitch McConnell cites figures to indicate that now that soft money was being abolished, this agreement would starve the parties, but he adds, astonishingly, "I intend to support the amendment." McConnell knows he's been whipped, and he doesn't like to lose roll call votes. In the end, the vote for the compromise is a huge victory for McCain, 84–16. Senators did what they're supposed to do: work together to resolve hard problems. But it was McCain who forced them into the position where they had to do it, and also enabled them to do it without anyone losing face. He had wrought a consensus on a difficult issue that also invited a lot of posturing. And, due to his persistence, the chemical change that the years-long campaign finance debate had undergone was now taking hold. On his way to an elevator after the vote, Joseph Lieberman remarked, "Isn't it incredible? People are voting for this for the most disparate reasons, but they're voting for it."

Coming off the Senate floor, McCain told the reform lobbyists who were encamped there, "We're stressing it's all severability."

Then, sitting on a bench in the reception room, McCain remarked to me, "You had real leadership in the room. Don Nickles said 'Let's split the difference between Feinstein and Thompson.' That was a very important factor, and I think there's a real desire to come to a conclusion on the bill. There was enormous force to get a bill. Thompson and Feinstein are highly regarded. I can't tell you exactly why it happened, but I knew there was going to be a point where it would either happen or not happen, and we were at that point.

"Mitch agreed because he didn't have the votes to win and he doesn't want another recorded vote that he lost. He's been very straightforward."

Referring to the bill's opponents, McCain said, "They're gonna pull out all the stops on nonseverability. They want to work on it overnight, and they may very well prevail. But I'm working it hard—on the floor, off the floor, talking to our supporters and everyone in the Senate. You don't know. They control the floor. There are people all over K Street trying to figure out amendments that can hurt this bill. So we still have a ways to go.

"I'm saying we still have some hurdles—severability, surprises, and final passage. You can't be sure of final passage because people are bothered by different sections of the bill."

In his office that evening, he warned his exuberant staff not to be overconfident. "Don't do that. I don't know where the votes are on severability. It's bad luck to do that."

Mark Salter said later that evening, "Our worst-case scenario used to be that we died on the Senate floor today." That could have happened had McCain not thrashed out an agreement on hard money, or if he'd ended up with a proposal that gave the Democrats an excuse to abandon the bill. Salter continued, "Now the worst case is that we lose on nonseverability and have to go to conference to knock it out." However, he had to admit, the fact that Daschle cooperated in getting an agreement on hard money was a sign that either the Democrats were in fact dealing in good faith or that Daschle didn't want them to walk away from the bill and be blamed for its defeat. Either way was fine with the McCain people.

After the meeting with his staff, McCain and his wife, Cindy (who had just returned from a charity trip to Morocco), went to dinner with Hagel and his wife, Lilibet. McCain invited Thompson, a lively conversationalist, along to help smooth the remaining tensions. But for all McCain's public protestations of his enduring friendship with Hagel, and his staff's assurances that he can compartmentalize, it seemed unlikely he'd forget a betrayal.

The great stakes that the opponents of reform had put on the non-severability proposal was a clear illustration of their weakened position. Their fallback position kept falling back. They'd considered filibustering the bill at the end but then figured that they didn't have the votes. Gradually, they realized that they might not be able to beat the bill in the Senate; that they might not be able to stop it in the House; that they might not be able to tie it up in a Senate-House conference; and even that the President might sign it. Bush had been sending out hints that he might. So their final fallback was to see to it that it was struck down in the courts.

A trade association lobbyist said on Wednesday afternoon, "They've given up on a filibuster—because they don't have the votes. Plus, after the whole thing has gone through no one wants to be the one who stands up and says, 'Let's kill it.' They say, 'Let DeLay kill it in the House.' " House Majority Whip Tom DeLay was already saying that he would do what he could to beat the reform bill in the House. But DeLay had said this in previous years and had been defeated, so it was not clear now how seriously his threat should be taken. Except that before, the House could count on the Senate to kill the bill. The lobbyist continued, "At this point, the last great hope is nonseverability, but the Republican leadership is very nervous about the vote on it. If they lose the vote on nonseverability, it's a slam dunk for the proponents of reform."

And now, on Thursday, March 29, near the expected end of the voting on the bill, and on the issue that worried McCain the most, the votes of several Democrats on nonseverability were still uncertain. Some had been saying that they were worried that if the bill wasn't made indivisible, a court could throw out the provision regulating electioneering ads and leave the soft money ban in place, with the result that large amounts of money would flow into the ads. This may have been a legitimate worry on the part of some, but there did seem to be a strong correlation between those who made the argument and those who were understood to be opposed to the bill. It was the last refuge for Democrats against the bill. McCain and his strategists had succeeded in throwing the spotlight on the doubters or potential deceivers. They had made deception more difficult.

They had gotten across the idea that a vote for nonseverability was a vote against reform.

In the Democrats' regular Tuesday caucus lunch, Daschle had made a strong argument against voting for nonseverability: "The vote on this is tantamount to winning or losing the whole fight on campaign finance reform." Robert Torricelli, of New Jersey, a former chairman of the Democratic Senatorial Campaign Committee, believed to be opposed to the bill, argued for nonseverability, saying that a court decision that struck down the curbs on electioneering ads but upheld the ban on soft money could leave a candidate defenseless against ads by outside groups. Playing on continuing resentments, he argued that the Democrats shouldn't put their political fates in the hands of the Supreme Court that had recently decided *Bush v. Gore.*

The McCain PAC web page and an e-mail alert to its roughly two hundred thousand e-mail correspondents listed seventeen senators of both parties whose votes were uncertain and asked that they be called (phone numbers supplied), not e-mailed (several Senate offices don't check their e-mail), and urged to vote against nonseverability. Taking a bank shot, McCain made a special effort to get support from Republicans from areas where the Christian right (which opposed the restrictions on ads), is strong. These people backed the soft-money ban but opposed the restrictions on issue ads, which might be more vulnerable to a court challenge. (If the bill were severable, perhaps the restrictions on ads would be struck down.)

At the principals meeting this morning, McCain said, "We've got to work everybody on severability. This can't be a cheap vote." He also urged his Democratic allies not to offer a string of amendments to the campaign finance bill in order to delay work on the budget. The Democrats threatening to do this were trying to play games against Bush. "We've got to move on," McCain said. "Let's not stall the inevitable."

Talking to reporters in the hallway outside the Senate chamber shortly before noon, John Breaux, who was opposed to the bill, said, "You can't have one part of the law struck down and the other part stand. It's ridiculous. I think a lot of Democrats feel that way and that a significant number are ready to vote for nonseverability."

At midday, William Frist, of Tennessee, chairman of the National Republican Senatorial Committee, offers the nonseverability amendment. Breaux is a co-sponsor. But McConnell is clearly in charge. In order to make the proposal more tempting, and in another fallback, it has been confined to the two main sections of the bill—the soft-money ban and the limits on electioneering ads wouldn't be severable—in the hope of attracting more votes. Now, not any little thing can bring down the whole law. Members of both parties are worried about ads, especially if the soft-money ban stands and the restrictions on ads don't.

Frist, sounding almost as if he supports the bill, which he doesn't, says, "McCain-Feingold has achieved a balance that we must be very, very careful not to disrupt."

Feingold calls on Thompson to speak. This has been choreographed. Thompson is well known as a former movie actor but he's also a former trial lawyer. He ticks off arguments against his fellow Tennesseean's amendment, speaking quietly, as good trial lawyers do. He points out that only one bill passed in twelve years contained a nonseverability clause. "Of 2,962 public laws," Thompson continues, "only one contained nonseverability." The courts have never ruled on a nonseverability clause, Thompson points out, "So we really are in uncharted waters."

In the reception room, McCain has come to talk to the reformers who've been patrolling the debate, gathering information, sometimes helping out in the drafting of amendments, and with the lobbying of senators: Don Simon, outside counsel of Common Cause; Meredith McGehee, vice-president of Common Cause; Trevor Potter, a former Republican chairman of the Federal Election Commission who is actually for reform and who advised McCain in his 2000 campaign; and Fred Wertheimer, who heads an organization called Democracy 21 and who has been an energetic catalyst for the bill. "Brownback's with us," McCain says, referring to Sam Brownback, Republican of Kansas, who is very closely allied with the Christian right. McCain's bank shot had partially paid off.

Offering his own analysis of the new version of nonseverability, McCain observes, "They have weakened their position by this. If the soft-money ban and Snowe-Jeffords [the electioneering-ad provision] go down in the courts, you're left with a bill that increases hard money. That should worry any Democrat."

On the Senate floor, Dick Durbin, of Illinois, who has been talking to reporters in a way that suggested that he's for nonseverability, makes a strong, substantive case for it, and then, turning on a dime, says he's prepared "to set aside my heartfelt concerns" and vote against it. Referring to *Gore v. Bush,* Durbin says that "our delicate balance of power has tipped in favor of the Supreme Court." John Edwards, widely considered a comer in Democratic politics, makes one of the best speeches of the entire debate. Edwards spent a fair amount of time preparing to rebut McConnell's perennial argument that proposed reforms were unconstitutional, but there hasn't been much of a debate on the constitutional issues. "This debate and this law is not about us," Edwards says. "It is not about what is good for Democrats, it is not about what is good for Republicans, and it is not about what is good for incumbent senators; it is about the American people. It is about whether their voice is going to be heard and whether they believe they have some ownership in their government."

Then McCain speaks. "We're now facing one of the major hurdles, perhaps the last major hurdle, before the resolution of this issue," he says. "If you vote for this amendment you are voting for soft money. That's really what this debate is about." Then he urges people to vote to table the amendment.

In the roll call, as is customary, only a few people vote at first, while others stream in from their offices and various meetings. The atmosphere on the floor is tense. Cheney is available if his vote is needed to break a tie. (In fact, he didn't leave Washington during this whole debate, in case he was needed.) As the roll call unfolds, there are several surprises. It appears close, but when Patty Murray, who now chairs the Democratic Senatorial Campaign Committee and was thought to be a possible vote for nonseverability, votes to table Frist's amendment, there's an audible gasp among the reformers on the floor. About two-thirds of the way through the vote, McCain and Buse know that their side has won. McCain leans on his lectern and smiles as the remaining senators come to the floor to vote. McCain and Lieberman give each other a thumbs up. While the vote continues, McCain goes to the well of the Senate, along with Thompson, to joke with Frist; they're not allowing hard feelings to settle in.

In the end, the vote isn't even close. The Senate has voted 57–43 against nonseverability, with twelve Republicans (not including Hagel) voting with McCain. Daschle, having worked hard on it all day, turned around the votes of several Democrats who had planned to vote for nonseverability. He's delivered. McCain's last big hurdle in the Senate has been overcome. It's over.

McCain, the supposed loner, the guy with the reputation for popping off, for not getting along with his colleagues, had done a remarkable thing—something that but for his sheer obstinacy, and also steadiness and heretofore unrecognized subtlety, wouldn't have happened. He forced the issue onto the Senate agenda, built a coalition, enlarged it, and guided it through treacherous waters. He got people who had never before supported campaign reform to support it. He remained disciplined and remarkably good-humored, holding his temper in check; he kept a steady strain. He reached out to long-time opponents, even sometime enemies—doing what he could to disarm them—as well as friends. He worked at keeping the debate on this most contentious subject—one on which every senator is an expert and in which contending forces have great stakes—civil. He turned out to be more longsighted, a shrewder strategist, a more sophisticated legislator than had been generally thought. This was a different man than the one in the earlier fights. He had learned and grown, and put that knowledge and growth to good use. He led.

In the radio-television gallery after the vote, McCain thanked several of his colleagues. "It's not over yet," he said. "There are still some amendments pending. We still have to get a bill, which I am guard-edly optimistic about."

He has to deal with the remaining amendments, many of them technical, tonight and tomorrow morning. He's still perturbed that the Democrats are playing games on the budget, fearing that it will upset the rhythm and momentum he's achieved. It opens up new uncertainty. He gives a live interview to Tom Brokaw and a taped one with *Nightline* as he shuttles back and forth to the Senate floor. Brokaw is in New York, and McCain, in the rotunda of the Russell Building, waits quietly, earpiece in ear, for Brokaw to ask him a question. He's experienced at this.

"Tom, I think the greatest concern, obviously, is to get it through the House, because now that we're shooting with real bullets, people will have a second look at it," McCain says. "So we're happy tonight, but we've still got a long way to go."

In McCain's office, his staff is giddy with success, and when McCain pops by on his way back to the floor from his *Nightline* interview, they give him a round of applause.

Sitting in a leather chair in his office, one foot propped on the coffee table, McCain responds, "We've got a long way to go, huh?" The staff laughs. This is the inside joke of the outside game. McCain allows himself to grin.

That evening, Lott set the final vote on the McCain-Feingold bill for late Monday afternoon. Also that evening, the Senate accepted an amendment by Levin to allow limited soft-money contributions to state party committees for voter registration and get-out-the-vote drives. A number of senators asked to co-sponsor the amendment, which was adopted by voice vote, as is done with noncontroversial proposals. Levin and McCain had been discussing the matter with the principals for two weeks—McCain agreed that the original bill was too restrictive, and he wanted to help Levin, who had been such a help to him. It seemed a minor matter at the time. But it turned out to be not a minor matter at all.

McCain was hearing a report that the House Republican leaders were threatening not to take up the bill.

Chapter 7

"There are some very brave people on both sides of the aisle."

O N THE LATE AFTERNOON of the following Monday, April 2, the Senate galleries are packed, which is unusual. What makes it particularly unusual is that everyone knows—at least in general terms—what the outcome of the roll call vote they have gathered to witness will be. But they have come to see an important event. Against what most people considered insuperable odds, the Senate is about to pass a bill that, if it became law, would be the most sweeping revision of the way political campaigns in this country are paid for since the post-Watergate reforms of 1974.

Not many senators are on the floor in the half-hour period allotted for debate before the vote, but more senators want to speak than there's time for. Mitch McConnell has passed out a chart purporting to demonstrate how the bill would damage the parties. Charles Schumer, of New York, in McCain's book one of the real troopers in the fight, says, "This is the Senate the Founding Fathers envisioned." When Paul Wellstone, who had caused McCain one of his most harrowing moments during the two-week debate, announces that though "I hate" part of the bill, he will vote for it, McCain, relieved, flashes him a wide smile all the way across the Senate floor. Wellstone gives him a "thumbs up."

McCain, closing the debate, thanks a number of senators, and says, "I asked at the start of this debate for my colleagues to take a risk for America. In a few moments, I believe we will do just that. Further, I will go to my grave grateful for the honor of being part of it."

When the roll is called, and those who missed the first calling of their name—which is, as usual, most of them—file by the clerks at the front of the chamber and state their vote, their expressions are revealing. A number of Democrats who had expressed strong misgivings about the bill, some of whom had been expected to oppose it if they could get away with it, vote "aye." Several do so with little enthusiasm. McCain, through his maneuvers all year but particularly in the past two weeks, has forced them into this situation. After a while, the floor becomes raucous. The senators have come through a long, potentially bitter, debate in a remarkably civilized manner, and now the suppressed tensions are being released. The roll call continues. Republican Party elders Richard Lugar, of Indiana, Ted Stevens, of Alaska, and Pete Domenici cast their first votes for campaign finance reform. Chuck Hagel quietly votes "no." Robert Torricelli passes by the front desk and, looking down unhappily, votes "aye." McCain's strategy of throwing the spotlight on the Democrats and keeping it there has worked. In the end, the vote for the new campaign finance bill is a strong 59–41. The McCain people had actually expected 60 votes for the bill, but the Republican leaders managed to hold back one vote.

Once again, McCain and his allies trooped to the radio-television gallery.

A reporter asked McCain, "Will you talk about how sweet a victory this is?"

McCain replied, "There are some very brave people on both sides of the aisle. Obviously, this is something we're very happy about. But the time we're going to pop a cork will be the day that the President of the United States signs this bill and that we are all together in the Rose Garden."

McCain leaves the gallery, goes down the marble steps and stops by the reception room to thank the reform lobbyists, who greet him with applause.

And then, on a balmy, pre-spring afternoon, he walks outside the Capitol and back to his office, a long train of cameras following him.

Chapter 8

**"The future takes care of itself if you do
your own work at the time."**

THE JOHN MCCAIN who had got the campaign finance reform
bill through the Senate was changing in other ways as well. He
was moving to a new place in American politics. He had learned,
politically and substantively, from the 2000 campaign, and from his
experiences since then, that the place from which he could be most
effective in American politics was the center. He hadn't set out to run
as a magnet for independent voters, but that's how things turned out.
He thought he was running as a Republican who would poke the
establishment in the eye—because that was his nature and his record.
Moreover, his campaign had begun amidst low expectations of how
far he could get. Independent voters flocked to him after New
Hampshire as well, but sometimes this occurred in states with closed
primaries, so the outcome wasn't affected.

The fact that in the general election neither Bush nor Gore
picked up on the McCain reform, shake-up-Washington themes, or
the McCain constituency, is one of the reasons both of them virtually
blew the election. This probably also contributed to Ralph Nader's
becoming a factor in the outcome.

At the end of the campaign, McCain and his advisers recognized that he had started something, and the question then was, What do we do with this?

In a highly unusual development, McCain lost the nomination fight but came out of the struggle with his national standing enhanced. He'd created a movement that sustained itself after the campaign. This was as much a surprise to McCain as it was to anyone else. He was at a new level.

In some ways, McCain isn't used to his new celebrity. He'll talk about how surprised he is that a certain well-known person knew who he was, or that an important government official has come to consult with him. But he knows the uses of his new standing in order to pursue his legislative goals.

Increasingly, McCain saw that there was a vacuum in American politics, a place for the growing number of people who don't identify with either party, or with conventional politics. The vacuum in American politics was the place that could have been occupied by a more stable Ross Perot, a Jesse Ventura without the feather boa and wrestling high jinks. It was the territory that Colin Powell seriously considered running a presidential race from in 1996—as a third-party candidate.

At the same time, McCain sought to be more effective in the Senate—and the nation. The closely divided Senate, and his new status, provided the opportunity.

And so he took a series of steps that began to define the new McCain centrism and that began to redefine him. This wasn't accidental. He was carving out a new place for himself—an exercise that wasn't without risks or misunderstandings. McCain's centrism was based on reform—an instinct that wasn't new to him. It wasn't the centrism of the averagers, those who try to place themselves in between two points of view and present themselves as the reasonable accommodators. Averagers don't develop followings.

McCain often identified himself with Theodore Roosevelt, a reformer. McCain's interest in TR had been developing over the past five years. He'd read Edmund Morris's first volume of Roosevelt's biography, *The Rise of Theodore Roosevelt.* When Roosevelt sent the "Great White Fleet" around the world to demonstrate that America was now a global power, McCain's grandfather was part of that fleet.

Closely associated with his identity as a reformer is the sense that McCain will "tell it like it is." Naming his campaign bus the Straight Talk Express had been a stroke of genius. McCain is a magnet for those tired of political double-talk, of trimmers. He knows that, and acts accordingly—mostly out of instinct. It would be folly for anyone else to try to mold himself into a "John McCain." His authenticity is a large part of his appeal.

By the summer of 2001, besides campaign finance reform, McCain had taken on the patients' bill of rights to regulate HMOs, a highly popular but for years unresolved issue in Congress. Though he joined the essentially Democratic side, led by Edward M. Kennedy and John Edwards, he had his own impact on the drawing up of the bill and was instrumental in getting it through the Senate in the summer of 2001. He took a stand on the President's tax bill that put him, almost alone among Republicans, against his party and his President. He held hearings on climate change; he concerned himself with adequate funding for national parks (in the tradition of Theodore Roosevelt). He joined with Joseph Lieberman on a proposal to close a loophole in the checks on people who buy guns at gun shows—an unusual position for a Republican Westerner. He joined with Chuck Schumer on legislation to provide consumers with greater access to generic drugs. He was also trying to stop gambling on college sports, a practice that was involving and, McCain believed, corrupting a large portion of student athletes—an issue which pitted McCain against the gambling industry.

Bush, by governing from the right in his first months in office, helped create the vacuum that McCain was now seeking to fill. McCain threw himself into the struggle over the patients' bill of rights, applying some of the lessons he'd learned from the campaign finance fight, most especially the benefits of getting others invested in the bill by having them sponsor amendments that were adopted. The bill was passed by the Senate in late June by a vote of 59–36. (When Bush threatened to veto the Senate bill, McCain issued a statement saying that he was "disappointed" but would "pledge my cooperation in any sincere effort to reach fair compromises on the outstanding issues that still divide us," but then he went on to take strong issue with some of the points in the President's veto threat.)

Having played a critical role in getting two major pieces of legislation through the Senate, McCain could no longer be called a maverick. Mavericks take unconventional positions, but almost by definition they aren't—can't be—effective legislators.

McCain is such an instinctive politician that one can miss the more ruminative side of his nature. He's also a serious reader of history. Beneath the cheerful scamp, the instinctive and occasionally impulsive (but less so than before) pol, the guy who enjoys a good political fight, was a man thinking through his role in American politics. It was something bigger and more thoughtful than figuring the angles on how to become President—a widespread preoccupation among senators. It wasn't that that possibility was totally absent from his thoughts or his discussions with advisers, but it wasn't *the* goal, the beginning and end, of his thinking.

Besides, given the number of things that had happened to him,

McCain was a fatalist, an existentialist without the angst. So while he entertained various possibilities, he mainly lived for the moment, for the fight at hand—though he did seem to be taking on more fights at a time, and they formed a pattern. They were issues more central to people's concerns than members of Congress's free parking perks at National Airport, which earlier in his Senate career McCain had unsuccessfully tried to remove.

Asked if he saw himself moving into a new space in American politics, McCain replied, "I don't know. I think if I do the best that I can, address the issues as best I can, the rest takes care of itself. The future takes care of itself if you do your own work at the time."

Some weeks McCain would attend the Republican moderates' Wednesday Group lunch, and some weeks he went to the Wednesday lunch of the Steering Committee, made up of conservative Republicans. In the spring of 2001, surveys showed that McCain's base was shifting: He was becoming extremely popular among Independents and Democrats, but dropping among traditional Republicans and conservatives.

When the President's tax bill was pending before the Senate in May, McCain offered an amendment to lower the top rate by a smaller amount and use the savings to give more relief to the middle class. Inevitably, some Republicans said he was showboating, but in fact this was his position during his 2000 campaign, in which he refused to outbid Bush (who had the mistaken impression that New Hampshireites would embrace his larger tax cuts). The amendment failed on a surprising 49–49 tie vote—the closest anyone had come to overturning the basics of the pending bill.

McCain then warned that if the final bill that came back from a House-Senate conference lowered the top rate any further from the Senate number (thirty-six percent), at the expense of the middle class, he would vote against the final bill; when it came back with a top rate of thirty-five percent, he did so. It was a bold thing to vote against the President's highest priority, and some of McCain's staff worried about the consequences for his standing within his party, but he decided to stick to his own beliefs.

McCain's heresy over the tax bill came amidst the turmoil on Capitol Hill over James Jeffords's decision, in late May, to switch from being a Republican to being an Independent. Jeffords's defection, brought about by the White House's mishandling him, by some of the hotheads in the Republican Conference bullying him, and by Trent Lott's failure to protect him, produced an earthquake, suddenly giving the Democrats control of the Senate and spawning all sorts of speculation as to who else might switch. The speculation inevitably turned to McCain.

And, as it happened, McCain had already invited Tom Daschle and his wife, Linda (whom McCain knew through her work as an aviation lawyer, and liked), to visit his ranch in Sedona the following weekend. This led to fevered talk that Daschle's visit meant that McCain might switch parties, but the invitation had been issued months before.

In fact, before the visit, Daschle and Kennedy had made a run at persuading McCain to switch parties, and some of his advisers, for whom the 2000 campaign had been a romantic adventure and the high point of their lives, were encouraging him to become an Independent. One McCain adviser set up an indirect line to Daschle through a Democratic cut-out. But McCain resisted making the switch. He had his base in Arizona and his role in campaign finance reform to protect. And McCain, with his conservative record on such issues as abortion, would never be welcome in the Democratic Party, and he's too conservative to feel comfortable in it.

McCain likes to invite couples to his ranch, often two at a time, thinking about the matchups. The McCains have their own cabin and three guest cabins. Democrats, including Feingold and Byron Dorgan, of North Dakota, and Republicans, including Hagel and Thompson, had visited his ranch. McCain once even invited Trent Lott, but that hadn't materialized. McCain enjoys socializing and showing off his ranch (taking guests on what Salter refers to as his "forced march") and shooting the breeze. He points out the fruit trees and loves to whip up his special barbecue sauce, and grill dinner. With the Daschles, it was mainly social, with a bit of trading insights about other people in the Senate. Senators don't get much time to socialize with each other in Washington anymore—largely because they're so busy raising money.

McCain was too practical, too much of a fatalist, too much of a realist, to engage in serious planning for another try at the Presidency so soon after the first one. When the subject came up in 2001, he dismissed speculation of what he might do in 2004. Much would depend on how Bush was doing three years hence. And on McCain's disposition after another couple of years. Besides, ballot restrictions in many states make running—and *winning*—as an Independent extremely difficult. ("If it were easy, a lot of people would have done it by now," says one McCain adviser.) And this time, he wouldn't begin with the low expectations of 2000. So his closest aides remained divided over whether another run was a good idea, and none of them knew where McCain would end up on the matter. Neither, it would appear, did McCain. But the private discussion in May of 2001 centered on switching parties, which McCain declined.

McCain had his staff prepare a statement to be issued when Jeffords formally announced his switch. The statement contained an indictment of how Jeffords had been treated and said, "Tolerance of dissent is the hallmark of a mature party, and it is well past time for the Republican Party to grow up." Some of McCain's colleagues wondered why he had to say such things. What they didn't understand was that the statement, which received a great deal of play in the press, was the very kind of thing that leads people to admire McCain for "telling it like it is"—and gives him power.

In fact, the events of that week, the news that the McCains were hosting the Daschles at their ranch, and a *Washington Post* story saying that McCain was discussing with his aides the idea of running for President as an Independent in 2004, threw White House aides into a frenzy. They called around to McCain's friends to see if they knew anything about what was behind all this. Bush called McCain at his ranch on Saturday. Bush noted that he'd been reading the papers. McCain assured Bush that he didn't plan to leave the party or mount a campaign for President. Not long after that, Bush's White House aides convened a meeting with some outside advisers to see how they could establish better relations with McCain, or at least keep him in the corral.

What they didn't understand was that McCain was not about flattery, or that where McCain could be helpful to the President, he wanted to be helpful to the President. (He *didn't* want to come off as Bush's Bobby Kennedy, and on some issues they did agree.) Where he differed, he was going to differ.

On June 5, the McCains had dinner with the Bushes at the White House, an event that had been postponed by mutual consent during the week of tumult and speculation set off by Jeffords's switch. It would only have caused more speculation. The evening, which began with drinks on the Truman Balcony, followed by chicken-fried steak, lasted eighty minutes. After chatting sociably about their families, about Arizona and Texas, and about events in Europe and the Middle East, the two men strove to find areas of agreement on policies. They agreed that the difficulties were between their advisers but not each other—which wasn't entirely the case. The President said that he wanted to work with McCain on the patients' bill of rights legislation. McCain replied, "We're not that far apart on HMO's, Mr. President." The President agreed.

McCain also suggested that he could help the President fight pork-barrel spending and win an enhanced military budget that included reform of the military structure. He was trying to get across to the President what he'd been saying all year—that there were issues on which he would support the President and try to help him. Not long after that, Karen Hughes, one of the President's closest advisers, went to Capitol Hill to have lunch with McCain in the Senate Dining Room—about as public a spot as could be chosen. McCain and Hughes had come to know each other during the campaign and had gotten along well.

During the same period, Karl Rove continued to consider McCain an inimical force, and he continued—even during Bush's diplomatic offensive—to trash McCain privately to reporters. Moreover, despite White House denials of earlier press stories saying that Rove had seen to it that people who had supported McCain in 2000 didn't get jobs in the Bush administration, instances of just that continued to occur.

McCain was privately upset about news stories suggesting he was thinking of changing parties and running as an Independent in 2004. He worried about not only breeding suspicions about his every act, and about making the gulf between himself and the White House wider than he wanted it to be (at least at this point), but also about what all this talk was doing to his conservative base, particularly in Arizona. The answer was that it was hurting it. His aides had him speak to the pollster John Zogby, whom McCain admired as being perhaps the most accurate in 2000 and who had been preaching the message that the country, by splitting as evenly as it did in 2002, had voted for centrism and moderation. Also, Zogby had made a study of independent voters, and felt that McCain had created a niche. He also believed that independent voters were becoming more moderate, leaning less to the left or right, and seeing John McCain as someone who could talk to them.

Zogby believed that McCain was right where the country was and that he was opening up the nation for a third party in the center. He thought that this explained McCain's prominence. Zogby also believed that McCain would always hold onto a portion of the right because he was a hero to them, and his own polling showed that McCain had a 56–20 favorable/unfavorable rating among the right, which was extremely high, and a 68–15 rating among independents. Zogby also believed that the talk of the possibility of McCain's running for President didn't hurt him "out there."

Still, McCain was worried about his home base. His staff publicly sloughed off a recall petition drive that was started in June as typical of the Arizona far right. It had been so down on Barry Goldwater after he retired from the Senate (he supported Bill Clinton's policy on gays in the military and criticized some leaders of the religious right) that some wanted to remove his name from the state Republican headquarters in Phoenix. The petition complained that McCain was disloyal to the President, especially in voting against his tax bill, and it also complained about his proposal to close the gun show loophole.

One form of the petition accused him of backing "dishonest and treasonist" legislation. Several of the petitions were posted at gun shops. The NRA was particularly angry with him for its being included in his campaign finance reform bill, at Wellstone's hand, and for trying to tighten a loophole in the gun control laws.

McCain himself was sufficiently concerned that he sent a four-page, single-spaced letter to every Republican precinct leader in Arizona, assuring them that reports that he might leave the Republican Party and possibly run for President as an Independent were "groundless." But he also argued that Republicans needed to reach out to suburban voters in order to be the majority party. He called for "greater tolerance" for Republicans "who occasionally dissent" from one or another majority position held by the party. He explained his vote against Bush's tax cut and talked about the need to build up national defense, about his work on the patients' bill of rights, and the gun show loophole. He also explained his invitation to Daschle to visit his ranch.

McCain's difficulty was that he was trying to bridge a wide chasm: to fill the vacuum at the center, work with the Democrats on some key issues, and not lose his conservative base. It was not an easy self-assignment, but not an impossible one for a man of McCain's stature and talents. At least, that's what he and his staff were gambling on.

If he were to decide to run, the machinery was in place. After the 2000 election, he and Rick Davis, his campaign manager, talked about his need to have some sort of infrastructure, which he had never had. At a minimum it would help him pursue his legislative interests—as well as explore the ramifications of his new-found political status. The campaign itself was a rather higgledy-piggledy affair. But since then he has had the PAC, Straight Talk America, headed by Davis, who now worked as a political consultant, and of which Weaver was the political director. The PAC, with 200,000 regular donors, funds McCain's travel for speeches and political appearances, and occasionally makes donations to other reform-minded politicians. Twice a year, the PAC holds a reunion for its most active members and highest donors.

McCain's own think tank, the Center for Conservative Reform, headed by Marshall Wittman, who's with the conservative Hudson

Institute, was established to work up policy papers on issues such as defense, and national service—an issue which McCain was planning to introduce in the fall. And he also established the Reform Institute, to work not only on campaign finance reform but also electoral reform—a large issue that grew out of perceived and real polling-place problems in 2000, and also one which could, as it happens, deal with the ballot difficulties erected by some states. Zogby does polling for the Reform Institute. This is quite a formidable infra-structure, and a sign of at least McCain's broadening interest and growing seriousness after 2000. It would of course be most handy were he to run for the Presidency.

The more McCain talked about Theodore Roosevelt as his hero—which he increasingly did—the more this raised the obvious question: Would he, like his hero, leave the Republican Party and run independently—as Roosevelt did in 1912 as the leader of the "Bull Moose" party? For all his protestations of noninterest in fol-lowing that route, McCain never completely slammed the door shut.

Chapter 9

"Let's get this done."

JOHN MCCAIN didn't trust the House Republican leaders. He didn't believe that they'd play it straight on the campaign finance bill. He assumed that they would try, one way or another, to kill it, and that they were being guided by Whip Tom DeLay, who was in fact meeting with outside groups opposed to the bill on ways to kill it. McCain figured that at a minimum, the House Republicans would stall on the measure, making it harder to get it through Congress by the end of the year.

As soon as the Senate passed the bill, McCain thought that the House reform leaders should initiate a procedure, called a discharge petition, which, if it gained the signatures of 218 members, or one more than half the House, would force the leaders to take up the bill, on terms laid out in the petition, and he urged this course on Christopher Shays. Twice before, House reformers had successfully used a discharge petition to force the Republican leadership to schedule debate on a campaign finance bill.

But Shays disagreed strongly. A leading supporter of reform, one of the very few House Republicans willing to go on the line for it year after year, to be the Republican co-sponsor of it, Shays had shown a lot of courage. But it wasn't in his nature to take on the leadership of his own party, in part because he trusted them and in part because he'd just as soon not take them on.

So Shays told McCain, and told his fellow reformers, that he had the word of House Speaker Dennis Hastert and of David Dreier, the chairman of the House Rules Committee, that there would be "no games" on the reform bill, that they would play fair. And he believed that they could be taken at their word. Shays, a highly decent man himself, assumed a certain decency on the part of people who gave him their word. Speaker Hastert, a former high school teacher and wrestling coach, was in fact a more benign figure than his predecessor, Newt Gingrich, and tried to be accommodating to the members of his flock and hold them together. Dreier, as chairman of the Rules Committee, which sets the terms for floor debate in the House, played a very important role—and he was an instrument of the House leadership.

Shays did worry very much that the House Republicans opposed to the bill would succeed at their strategy of getting it to a conference with the Senate and burying it there. McCain was less worried about this—or so he seemed for a while. He felt that it wouldn't be politically supportable to bury the bill in conference once it had been passed by the Senate and the House. Shays, far less combative than McCain, worried that McCain actually relished the idea of a fight to get the bill out of conference. But in the end, McCain was a key participant in a difficult effort to get a bill before the House that was as close as possible to the Senate bill, so that the Senate could simply take it up and agree to it.

With Tom Daschle now the Majority Leader, that prospect had become more likely. Such a motion would be subject to a filibuster, but McCain and his allies believed that they could break such a filibuster. Some parliamentary tactics are technically feasible but not politically sustainable, and McCain believed it simply wouldn't be politically sustainable for opponents to kill by filibuster a campaign finance reform bill that had been passed by the House and the Senate.

In late May, McCain went over to Minority Leader Dick Gephardt's office, on the House side of the Capitol. He had asked for the meeting with Gephardt, in part to send a message to the House and Senate Republican leaders that there was a powerful coalition behind the reform bill. McCain could have simply made a phone call, but word of the meeting was likely to get around, as it did. After some pleasantries, with each man complimenting the other on what he had done for campaign finance reform, McCain said, "I want to work with you. I'll do anything I can." Gephardt said he wanted to work with McCain and that he thought he could hold almost all of his Democrats.

McCain was unhappy that the House leaders hadn't set a specific date for the debate. In mid-May, Hastert, responding to public opinion and the pressures brought by McCain, had written to Shays, saying, "It is my intent that we bring the matter to the floor in early July, after we return from" the Fourth of July recess. McCain didn't find that specific enough. He told Gephardt that he still thought that a discharge petition effort should be started. Gephardt agreed, but Shays didn't, so this was a moot issue at that point.

Gephardt and McCain also talked about how to alleviate the concerns of the thirty-seven-member Congressional Black Caucus, many of whose members were insisting that they needed soft money for get-out-the-vote drives. Word of this discussion, as intended, would get back to the Black Caucus.

McCain told Gephardt that they seemed to be in agreement on everything. A strong alliance was forming, and would soon be joined in war.

There was some speculation, especially on the part of outside reformers, that Gephardt and other House Democratic leaders, hav-

ing had a free ride in previous years, since they could pass reform legislation and count on the Senate to kill it, didn't really want to pass it
this time. But McCain had decided that Gephardt was genuinely trying to get a reform bill, and so he trusted him.

Gephardt was working with less promising numbers this time
around; almost half the Republicans who had supported reform in
the past hadn't returned to this Congress. Several of their replace-
ments might also support reform, but he couldn't be sure. The House
Republican leadership had made a special effort, called Battleground
2000, raising a special fund to get new Republicans elected, which
made them subject to considerable pressure from the leadership.

Gephardt was counting on McCain to help get enough House
votes to pass the bill. A House Democratic leadership aide said, "The
atmosphere is different this year. McCain isn't going to give up. Anyone who says that the House Democrats won't support reform hasn't
been paying attention. Democrats don't want McCain going around
attacking them in their districts." He added—and this was an aide
who started out the year angry with McCain, whom he held responsible for the fact that the Republicans had retained control of the
House—"The big difference is McCain. We've never before had such
a big figure with such a commitment to a piece of legislation, willing
to take on his President and his party." Shays, too, despite their differences over tactics, saw McCain as the "trump card."

But some House Democrats were balking at being told that they
should simply accept the Senate bill. It was a matter of institutional
pride—and also a convenient way to slide away from supporting the
bill. These Democrats would be reminded—by Marty Meehan,
Shays's co-sponsor, among others—that they'd supported reform in
the past and wouldn't look good abandoning it now that it counted.
But some had substantive objections to the Senate bill, and these
would have to be thrashed out before the bill came to the House
floor.

McCain was prepared to play his outside game again, and he would keep talking to the local media who called for interviews. He was planning to remind those Republican House members for whom he had campaigned of their agreement to support reform. Some of the commitments were more specific than others; only a dozen or so said they'd actually support the Shays-Meehan bill.

McCain was in fact in a delicate situation with regard to the House. There was little historical precedent for a member of one chamber to be presumed to have so much influence on the other—an influence that not everyone in that other chamber appreciates.

Meanwhile, McCain had yet another fight to make within his own chamber. By mid-May—after forty-three days—Trent Lott hadn't sent the campaign reform bill over to the House, usually a routine matter. McCain suspected that this was part of the Republican plot to delay action on the bill, or at least to interrupt its momentum.

Following futile talks between McCain aide Mark Buse and Lott's staff, McCain took the issue to the Senate floor, confronting Lott directly. "The holding of this bill is completely arbitrary and patently unfair," McCain told the Senate. And on a roll call on a resolution by McCain instructing that the bill be sent to the House without delay, the vote was 61–36, a stronger vote than even for passage of the bill. A Lott spokesman said afterward that McCain was trying to "coerce" the House, but a few days later Lott said that he would send the bill to the House. By this time the House leadership had said that the bill would definitely come up right after the July 4 recess.

The House Republican leaders were playing it smarter this year than in the past. DeLay receded from a public role (he had once said that

didn't have much margin for changes in the Senate bill. In and around his efforts in the Senate to pass the patients' bill of rights, McCain met with some House Republicans to urge them to support the bill. He was worried that the outside pressure that had existed before the Senate took up the bill wasn't there for the House bill.

The soft money issue was more difficult, because the outside reformers now realized that the Levin amendment would allow a donor to give ten thousand dollars to each party unit within a state—for example, each county committee—which could add up to quite a large contribution. As the reformers saw it, this reopened the soft-money loophole. McCain and Buse didn't think that this was a real-world problem—that the giving of such money wasn't likely to influence a member of Congress. McCain said at one of the meetings, "I don't think this is as big a problem as some people perceive it. If we can fix it in a way that makes Carl and Sander [Levin, Carl's brother and a congressman from Michigan] happy, let's do it. But I don't think it's a big problem." McCain's real concern was that the attempt to preconference the bill might come at the cost of loss of support in the Senate. This took constant balancing. In one meeting, McCain said, "Look, we can't be significantly changing this bill. It passed by a large margin, and we need to keep the bill as close to the Senate's as possible."

Meanwhile, members of the Black Caucus were telling Gephardt that the Levin amendment wasn't sufficient to meet their concerns about having enough soft money for get-out-the-vote drives, and Gephardt was telling McCain that—despite the opposition of some reformers and House liberals—some form of the Levin amendment was necessary to get their votes. Meehan agreed. But reformers in and out of the Congress were unhappy.

McCain was willing to help Gephardt out on this. Meehan, too, asked for McCain's help on it—which he had done on other occasions as well. Also, McCain felt obliged to Levin for his overall help on the bill.

But each attempt to tighten the Levin amendment to satisfy reformers succeeded in angering Black Caucus members. And the reformers received a serious blow when, at the end of June, Albert Wynn, of Maryland, and the head of the campaign finance reform task force of the Black Caucus—despite being implored by Gephardt not to do it—signed on as a co-sponsor of the Ney bill.

Actually, the Black Caucus itself was divided. John Lewis, a hero of the civil rights movement, to whom McCain had spoken, was in favor of the bill. "It's the right thing to do," he said. Lewis told McCain he could support the Senate-passed bill. And Harold Ford, of Tennessee, also a member of the Black Caucus, was pointing out publicly that more soft money is spent on administrative costs and phones than on get-out-the-vote drives. In fact, two House Democrats close to the Black Caucus said some members of the Black Caucus liked to be able to distribute large sums of soft money so that people would be beholden to them, and see them as in positions of power. One said, "Some individuals see this as their source of power not just in Congress but in the black community nationwide."

The pressure was on to get the House version of the reform bill drafted before the July 4 recess. "Let's get this done," McCain urged them. "Let's get this done."

McCain and Buse thought that their House counterparts, having passed bills relatively easily in the past, weren't as accustomed as they were to the viciousness of opponents of reform, that they didn't realize what they were in for.

· · ·

On Sunday, July 1, Hastert, appearing on *Meet the Press,* charged that McCain, by sending letters to twenty-four Republicans he had campaigned for, reminding them of their pledge to support reform, was "bullying" House members. There was no overt threat in McCain's letters, but perhaps a less-than-subtle suggestion. They contained a boilerplate paragraph about how "invigorating" it was "to travel across America, campaigning for you and other Republicans, and feel the incredible, energetic support for reform"; and then a pointed reminder, as in, "Felix, I especially remember the event we did together at the school town hall meeting in Riverhead, N.Y., on April 15. And I remember our personal conversations about our shared passion for reform." And then, "Now you have the opportunity to fulfill the campaign promise you and I made together on the stage in Riverhead."

Hastert's language about McCain was uncharacteristic and suggested that he was planning to take a more aggressive role than before—and, possibly, that he was under pressure from DeLay. The obvious purpose was to make McCain the issue, rather than the Republicans' own efforts to defeat the reform bill—to try to diminish McCain's effectiveness.

The following Sunday, only days before the bill was to be brought up, McCain said on *Face the Nation,* "Let's be clear. If this loses, it will be because of the efforts of the House Republican leadership."

Chapter 10

"Chris, it's not Denny, it's Tom DeLay."

THE WEEK that the bill was to come before the House didn't begin well for the reformers. Hastert had set the debate for the Thursday after the July 4 recess, July 12. The House leaders hoped to dispense with it in one day, to prevent pressure to pass it from building, as it had in the Senate.

On Monday, McCain, Feingold, Shays, and Meehan held rallies for the bill in New York, at Theodore Roosevelt's boyhood home, and in Boston, at Faneuil Hall. New York was chosen because of its large media market, and Theodore Roosevelt's home because McCain often points out that it was under TR, in 1907, that corporate contributions to federal candidates were made illegal. Boston was less necessary in terms of getting the bill through the House, but Meehan, enmeshed in a nasty redistricting fight, had asked McCain to hold an event there, and that was good enough for McCain. The events didn't get much attention because the news organizations were focused on the scandal involving Gary Condit, the congressman from California who had had an affair with an intern who had later disappeared, and on a shark attack on an eight-year-old boy off the coast of Florida.

. . .

The Republicans were working their members hard, especially the freshmen, reminding them of the leaders' financial help. Two powerful unions, the American Federation of State, County and Municipal Employees, and the UAW, had come out against the bill. The NRA was targeting Democrats from pro-gun districts and warning that a vote for Shays-Meehan would be held against them. The National Right to Life Committee was telling members that the vote on Shays-Meehan would be counted (negatively) on their scorecard of members' voting records.

And, despite the fact that the Shays-Meehan bill was supposed to be completed before the July 4 recess, Gephardt, still scouting for votes, was continuing to propose changes, which led to a new crisis within the reform movement. Daschle, too, wanted some last-minute changes. It could be argued that these people should have had their effort pulled together by this time, but that's not the nature of Congress. It tends not to focus on things until it absolutely has to. Moreover, Daschle had just taken over as Majority Leader and was preoccupied with other subjects. This wasn't the only matter on Gephardt's agenda, either. And if a significant number of the Black Caucus members are holding out for as much as they can get before pledging their vote, as was happening, the appeasement process goes on. But the appeasement can't take place in a vacuum.

Gephardt, reaching for as many Black and Hispanic Caucus votes as possible, wanted to raise the aggregate amount of hard money that people could contribute in a two-year election cycle to well above the Senate's figure of seventy-five thousand dollars. But many reformers were unhappy to see the amount go to six figures, as Gephardt was proposing. Also, to mollify the Black Caucus, Gephardt wanted to allow federal party officials to raise the soft money under the Levin amendment.

At an afternoon meeting in Daschle's office on the Tuesday after the recess, the reform leaders of the two chambers seemed to go along. But Don Simon, Common Cause's outside counsel; Fred Wertheimer, head of Democracy 21; and Meredith McGehee of Common Cause decided that things had gone too far and marched over to see Feingold and McCain to protest, and threatened to withdraw their support of the bill. They argued that allowing national party officials to raise soft money under the Levin amendment would take the system back to having the politicians reward large donors and that the hard-money aggregate shouldn't get into six figures. (McCain was busy on the floor, so they carried out their anger on Buse, who didn't appreciate their attitude.)

McCain thought they had a point and said in a meeting early that evening in Gephardt's office that the hard-money aggregate should be held at ninety-five thousand dollars and that party officials shouldn't be allowed to raise the soft money. He had checked with Fred Thompson, who had been instrumental in setting the lower Senate figure, and Thompson said that while he wasn't happy with this new figure, he wasn't going to "tear up the sheets" over it. He wasn't going to make things difficult for his buddy McCain. McCain told the House reform leaders he'd defend the ninety-five-thousand-dollar figure in the Senate: "I'll take the heat for it, I'll explain it to people." But at the same meeting, both McCain and Feingold told the House reform leaders that it was time to stop making changes to the Senate bill.

Don Simon and two congressional staff members didn't finish drafting the changes until one A.M. on Wednesday, the day that the Rules Committee was to meet to set the rule for the debate to begin on Thursday.

Because of the House's large size (435 members) and capacity for chaos, the Rules Committee sets the time limits for debate, dictates which amendments will be in order, how much time is allowed for debate on each of them, and the sequence of the votes. A rule is a highly political instrument and can affect the outcome.

Shays asked the Rules Committee to allow that all of the last-minute changes, fourteen altogether, some of them technical, be offered en bloc, subject to one up-or-down vote, which was fairly routine.

At that point, Gephardt thought that he could get 190 to 195 Democratic votes for the Shays-Meehan bill, and Shays thought he could get thirty Republicans. But the minimal presumed total of 220 wasn't enough to relax about (218 votes were necessary), and Gephardt continued to work the Democrats for more votes. At one meeting, he pointed to a news report saying that House Republicans had set a record in fundraising for the current election cycle and warned his colleagues that they would be "buried in soft money" unless they supported reform.

On Tuesday, McCain called three House Republicans who were on the fence; his Straight Talk America website and e-mails identified wavering congressmen and asked that they be called.

The Republicans saw their opportunity, and they took it. They realized that the coalition in favor of the bill was fragile and that the reformers were still scrambling for votes by adding amendments. A possible, perhaps likely, way to try to break the coalition apart was to require separate votes on each of the fourteen amendments; if even one or two failed, there might not be enough votes for the reformers' bill.

Gephardt understood this. One amendment, inserted at the last minute at the behest of the Black Caucus, removed a restriction on the Levin soft-money provision. If that change was defeated, which was possible in a separate vote, Gephardt might not have enough votes to pass the bill. Republicans opposed to reform were perfectly capable of voting with purist reformers in order to cause trouble—as had happened in the Senate on the Wellstone amendment.

On Wednesday afternoon, the day before the bill was to come to the House floor, word circulated that the Republicans, through their control of the Rules Committee, would require separate votes on each of the fourteen new amendments. David Dreier, the committee's chairman, had been told that if he didn't do this, the seventy-two-member conservative Republican bloc in the House, the Conservative Action Team (now called the Republican Study Group but still referred to as the CATs) would rebel. The CATs are very close to DeLay, and, like him, opposed the bill. They saw the rule as a way to kill it. And Drier wasn't an independent figure.

Their threat was serious because if the CATs did indeed oppose the rule on the House floor, that would make Hastert dependent upon a large number of Democrats to get the rule adopted, and a Speaker doesn't want to rely on the opposition party to put across a rule. The tribal customs surrounding a rule for debate are only partially connected with the substance of the issue at hand.

Gephardt decided that the rule must be defeated. (The last time the Rules Committee had done such a thing was in 1981, when the Democrats controlled the House, and that rule was defeated.) He already had a great deal else on his hands—including eight poison pill amendments, Republican amendments that might end in killing the bill. The difficulty of having to whip and explain and win each of the additional fourteen changes was as clear to Gephardt as it was to the Republican leadership. One of the Democratic Whips said, "It was too questionable to try to win the fourteen votes. It was hard enough to whip the bill—a lot of members were being coy."

Shays was reluctant to try to defeat the rule—it's a very hard thing to ask members to go against their leaders on such a question. On Wednesday night, continuing into Thursday morning, he was ambivalent, sometimes thinking that the rule should be defeated, sometimes thinking the reformers should try to win the fourteen amendments separately. He thought that the rule couldn't be defeated. And without the support of Shays, the leading House sponsor of the reform bill, the rule in fact probably couldn't be defeated.

Gephardt called McCain. "The way it's structured we can't hold our people together," he told him. "So we have to defeat the rule." Gephardt also argued that the rule was unfair.

"Of course," McCain replied. And he went into full battle mode. McCain called Meehan and said, "We've got to get a fair shot here," and told him that he was going to get some House Republicans together.

Around 6:00 P.M., Lindsey Graham, a South Carolina Republican who had become a close friend of McCain's (he was one of two South Carolina members of Congress with the courage to back McCain in the primary there); Mark Kirk, a freshman from Illinois whom McCain had campaigned for; Zach Wamp, a Tennesseean who had supported reform; and Shays met in McCain's office. Various strategies were discussed, and it wasn't clear at that point that the reformers could defeat the rule. One of the purposes of the meeting was to shore up Shays against the rule. Later, McCain phoned Shays to encourage him further, but Shays remained ambivalent.

There wasn't a lot of communication between the baby-faced, slow-talking, folksy, forty-six-year-old Graham and Gephardt's office, because Graham had been one of the leaders of the impeachment move against Clinton. In fact, the reason Graham backed McCain in the primaries in 2000 was because he thought he'd be "the perfect anti-Clinton." Recently, for the second year in a row,

Graham had spent the July 4 holiday with the McCains at their ranch in Arizona—this time along with Warren Beatty and Annette Bening, Joe and Hadassah Lieberman, and assorted children.

Graham, now running for the Senate to succeed Thurmond, had supported campaign finance reform in the past—as unusual for a South Carolina Republican as being for John McCain—and had put together a coalition of Bush and McCain Republicans in his state. He worried that McCain had alienated his conservative base. "The thing about John McCain," Graham said, "is that if you ever get to be his friend, he'll be with you thick and thin. There ain't a lot of that up here."

Thursday morning, the day of the scheduled House debate, McCain went through his usual morning routine of reading the papers while he drank a cup of cappuccino, which aides get from a shop in the basement of the Russell Building. At 8:00 he went into Salter's office to discuss strategy. Weaver and Salter had gone over a list of people they thought he should call about the rule. Because of the crisis, Salter had ordered Ives to cancel some radio interviews planned for that morning, so that McCain could call House members to urge them to defeat the rule and to support the Shays-Meehan bill.

In the course of the early-morning calls, McCain learned that the reason he couldn't reach a number of people was that a group of moderate House Republicans, the Republican Main Street Partnership, was holding an event at the Capitol Hill Club, a Republican redoubt a few blocks away from the Russell Building. He grabbed Weaver and jumped in his car to drive over there to do some buttonholing. On the way, he spotted Benjamin Gilman, a Republican from New York, and got out of his car to try to persuade him.

Later that morning, on his way to a press conference with some conservative House Democrats (the "Blue Dogs") to urge defeat of the rule, McCain said, "When Gephardt tells me he thinks we won't win if we have to vote on all fourteen amendments, I take him at his word."

At the press conference, Shays, answering a question he would clearly rather not have been faced with, said, "With this rule the House Speaker has broken his promise to be fair. I had a distinguished senator say we were going to get screwed, and I said no." Then he looked down and said, sadly, "He was right."

To break the tension, McCain joked, "I never used such language."

On the way out of the gallery, McCain remarked, "Chris said 'Denny is a fair man.' I said, 'Chris, it's not Denny, it's Tom DeLay.' "

A fight over a rule in the House is unlike any other: The blood lust of the House is roused. It's a very big thing for a Speaker to lose a rule; Hastert hadn't lost one since he became Speaker in early 1999, after the fall of Newt Gingrich. For the Democrats, who felt that the Republicans had mistreated them in this Congress in several respects, this became an issue of the rights of the minority. So a rules fight becomes extremely partisan, and Shays wasn't wrong in his sense that it was a hard thing for a member of the Speaker's own party to vote against him.

Some of the reform forces, including Gephardt, understood all day that the risk of defeating the rule was that there would be no bill—this was a matter of risk assessment, with no definitive answers. A close ally of Gephardt said later, "We anticipated that if we defeated the rule, the Republicans would go away, but we believed that they would have to bring the bill back, just as there was pressure on them to bring it up now."

By midday, relations between Shays and McCain's office had

deteriorated. The McCain people had been instrumental in setting up a separate whip system around Shays, to work on defeating the rule; it included Lindsey Graham and other Republicans who supported reform. McCain asked that they keep him informed and let him know if they needed him to do anything. Graham, hearing of separate negotiations between Shays and Dreier, called Salter. "You better get over here. This thing is going nowhere quick." McCain rushed over to the House side of the Capitol. The meeting ended up in Gephardt's office, room H 204.

Gradually, seven moderate Republicans, including Shays, arrived, and a little later so did Gephardt, from another meeting with the Black Caucus. He met with the Caucus twice that day, negotiating over how much money would be spent in their districts on get-out-the-vote drives. One time he had Daschle in tow to assure them that the party committees would come up with the necessary resources for get-out-the-vote drives. Gephardt had tried to tell the Caucus that its constituency couldn't possibly come out ahead in the policies that result from the soft-money system, which was true enough, but beside the point for some members.

The point of this meeting was to give Gephardt a chance to tell the Republican reformers why he had problems with the rule. He said he could get 190 votes, "but not if I have to go through fourteen hoops." He also said that he objected to the Republicans' breaking the amendments into three or four packages, as Dreier was now suggesting to Shays, on the grounds that it's the minority's right to present its own alternative.

The moderate Republicans complained about the Republican leadership's game-playing on the rule. The consensus was that if the rule was voted down, Hastert would offer an alternative one. Some thought that if the bill was killed for now because of the rule, there would be a backlash that the Republican Party would have to deal with and the bill would be brought back up. McCain, summing up the consensus, said, "I think we should defeat the rule. It's not a fair procedure." And then he went around the room asking, "Is this okay with you?" It was unanimous.

Upon emerging from Gephardt's office, McCain was asked by reporters who had discovered the meeting if they had decided to go ahead and defeat the rule. Evading the question, he said, cheerfully, "Another meeting in a round of meetings." He was trying to be careful; it wasn't for him to be announcing what the House members were going to do. Shays came out of Gephardt's office looking troubled.

A few minutes later, I encountered Tom DeLay coming off the House floor.

Asked, if the rule was defeated what would happen next, DeLay, breaking into a broad grin, replied, "Nothin'."

Chapter 11

"It's impossible to keep it off the floor of the House of Representatives."

DENNIS HASTERT apparently wasn't aware of DeLay's strategy, and he wasn't interested in losing a rule for the first time. So, when a delegation of Republicans from the meeting in Gephardt's office went to tell him that the votes existed to defeat the rule, he wasn't happy but was willing to deal. Hastert bristled that he was being "blackmailed," but added, "I can count." So, he said, the reformers could have their fourteen amendments en bloc.

Shays, in an effort to help Hastert save face, suggested that Ney, who was also at the meeting, should be allowed to offer a new amendment. Ney hadn't made such a request; in fact he had no amendment to offer. Shays said later, "I was trying to find a fair thing and for Denny not to totally have to reverse himself." This well-intended if, under the circumstances, misplaced sense of fairness played a large part in the subsequent calamity.

On the House floor, Gephardt wound up a speech against the rule. "I hope that we can still have a rule today that's fair . . . A vote for the rule as it presently reads is a vote against real campaign finance reform." The word had already spread on the Republican side of the aisle that "Denny has caved," and when the conservative Republicans saw Shays go up to Gephardt to relay what he had worked out with Hastert, they worked themselves into a rage. The CATs were furious. Word had also traveled that McCain, whom they were none too fond of anyway, had been at a meeting in Gephardt's office! And now there was the sight of Shays conferring with the opposition leader. Of course, Gephardt, as the Minority Leader, had to be consulted. That these reactions were largely irrational was beside the point. At issue was control of the House. The conservative Republicans, opposed to the bill anyway, were now in rebellion against their own leader for offering a deal on the rule.

Someone in Gephardt's entourage said that they would need three hours to study the Ney amendment and to whip the Democratic caucus on it. Shays, confronted with Gephardt's demand for time, sought out Barney Frank, a Massachusetts Democrat and one of the smartest members of the House. Frank is the head of the Democrats' parliamentary group, which works to ensure that the minority's rights are being protected on the House floor. Frank suggested that Gephardt needed only two hours, to which Gephardt agreed, and then Frank suggested an hour and a half—and that that need consume no extra time on the bill because the discussions of the Ney amendment could take place while general debate on the bill was going on. Ney, whom Shays had brought into the discussion, was bewildered since he didn't yet have an amendment to show anyone. Ney said to Shays, "Chris, they want to see my amendment; I don't even know what I'm going to do." The whole argument had an element of the absurd.

The anger on the Republican side made it clear to other members of the Republican leadership that Hastert's deal was unacceptable to their side, which was as they wished—so, while the discussions over how much time to spend on the nonexistent Ney amendment were proceeding, they called a party conference, the clear purpose of which was to kill Hastert's deal.

Lindsey Graham said, "The Republican leadership was looking for a way out and they took Gephardt's hesitation to be 'no.' There was no real effort to work this out."

By the time Frank came up with his solution, the enraged Republicans had left the floor to convene the party conference in a room in the basement of the Capitol. Once that happened, Gephardt's people knew that there would be no deal on the rule.

In a long and heated meeting of the House Republican Conference, both McCain and Shays were attacked. Amo Houghton, of New York, a scion of the Corning Glass family, said later, "That conference was Stillman's gym—it was a locker room kind of thing." J. D. Hayworth, of Arizona, one of the more obstreperous members of the Republican Conference, likened Shays's action to that of the appeaser Neville Chamberlain. There was much talk of how the Republicans had been "stabbed in the back." It was asked: How dare McCain try to influence members of our conference? Majority Leader Dick Armey, of Texas, called McCain "arrogant" and "pompous." He accused Shays of treating with the enemy.

Many House Republicans were already angry with McCain for having voted against the President's tax bill and for siding with the Democrats on the patients' bill of rights. Members of the House and the Senate frequently try to pressure each other, but McCain presented both a big fat target and also a threat. Hastert told the conference that he had tried to be fair to Shays, but that Gephardt had rejected his offer.

Afterward, much discussion arose over whether Gephardt should have simply accepted Hastert's proposal at once, since this turned out to be—or seemed to be—the pivotal moment of the day. The problem, as Gephardt and his people saw it, and some detached Democrats back them up, was that, first, they didn't know what was in the Ney amendment (which they couldn't since it didn't yet exist), and, second, that it was likely to contain tricks to try to win over a patch of Democrats here or there—perhaps some members of the Black or Hispanic caucuses—and that it would in fact take time to study and whip.

There was some later muttering among reformers that perhaps Gephardt had opposed the rule and then hesitated on the Hastert deal in order to kill the bill—that he didn't really want campaign finance reform. But this flew in the face of Gephardt's strenuous efforts in the days and hours leading up to the House consideration of the bill.

All of this maneuvering was about very big stakes—for many and very big interests. It was about preserving the current shambles of a money system and the status quo; about allowing well-heeled individuals and interests to buy influence through big contributions; about permitting business interests, labor organizations, and other interest groups to keep spending soft money to support or defeat candidates. It was about ridding the campaign finance system of some of its worst excesses.

There was nothing for McCain to do about the events in the House during the non-negotiations with Gephardt and then the Republican conference, so he went about his Senate business. On the Senate floor, he continued his battle against what he considered pork-barrel spending, in this case a proposed appropriation of two million dollars to restore an iron statue of Vulcan, the Roman god of fire and iron, in Birmingham, Alabama. One and a half million dollars had already been spent on the $12.5 million project. "While the federal surplus is dwindling, why should federal dollars pay for a face-lift of a statue of a Roman god in Alabama?" McCain asked the Senate. He lost, by a vote of 87–12, but he was content to make his point. McCain has long opposed "pork-barrel spending" on the merits, but he also uses the issue as a symbol people can understand about what's wrong with Washington.

Shortly after five, the House Republicans returned to the floor, and it soon became clear that they intended to let the reformers vote down the rule, and then they'd call it a day. Hastert wasn't allowed to cave. It had become one of the strangest days in recent memory in the House, filled with emotional highs and lows. In the end, the opponents of reform succeeded in tricking the reformers, as McCain had feared.

Graham had called McCain and told him that the conference had been rough, and they began to discuss calling the group back together to decide what to do. Moments later, he called again and said, "They're voting." DeLay's plan to let the reformers vote down the rule and have that be the end of the matter was now in effect. At that point, McCain and his aides realized that there was nothing left for the reformers to do for the moment but defeat the rule.

Watching the House vote in his office, McCain cheered on the reformers as they defeated the rule. It was important to show strength for the fights to come. He was reluctant to leave until he saw the final total but was urged by his aides to get over to the House side, where a press conference would be held following the vote.

The rule was defeated by a vote of 203–228, with nineteen Republicans voting to defeat it. In a clear sign of the leverage the Republican leadership had over their freshmen, only one—from a district that neighbors Shays's in Connecticut—voted against the rule; he had received dispensation from DeLay, who was playing the very behind-the-scenes role McCain had envisioned and other Republicans in the leadership were trying to keep hidden.

All the Democrats but one voted to kill it. The Democrats deliberately didn't applaud when they won the vote; they wanted to keep the onus on the Republicans. The House leadership quickly made it clear in a floor colloquy that they would now move on to other issues. Hastert said afterward that he had "no plan to bring up this bill." His press secretary issued a statement saying, "the biggest proponents of campaign finance reform, Chris Shays and John McCain, were the first to stab the bill to death."

Hastert hadn't had a good day; he was confronted by both sides of his conference, and in both cases lost.

In Gephardt's office, McCain asked, characteristically: "OK, what's next?" He was told that some Republican moderates had called and said that they'd hold a press conference on what had happened, but they didn't want Gephardt to be there. They'd just committed treason against their leadership.

McCain turned to Gephardt and said, "Maybe we should just do this with Republicans, Meehan, and Feingold."

Gephardt replied, "Whatever works."

The press conference, in the House radio-television gallery, is a solemn affair. The reform sponsors are still coming to grips with what has happened. The reform bill, which they had become increasingly convinced they could win today, is now in abeyance at best. Standing back in a corner, McCain, for once, looks glum; his lips tightly pressed together and his brows furrowed, he stares at the floor. (Outside the gallery, the reform lobbyists look stricken.)

After the others have their say, McCain speaks in a quiet voice. "I hope when things cool off, as they will over the weekend, we can negotiate consideration of this bill next week. I do, believe it or not, have sympathy for the Republican leadership." He's trying to be the peacemaker, or to appear so. He knows, as do his allies, that a discharge petition would be time-consuming and that even if they succeed in getting enough signatures, they won't be able to get the bill back before the House until at least the fall. Congress is scheduled to be in recess during August. But McCain is also laying the groundwork for a discharge petition, if it becomes necessary, without appearing to be carrying on a war. "I don't want to have to think about a discharge petition," he says. He hopes "we can put the discomfort behind us."

McCain wasn't doing his usual determined, cheerful, "We'll be back" routine.

After the press conference, McCain headed over toward the Senate floor. "It was an important vote," he said, "because if we didn't beat the rule it was over. It was Gephardt's assessment, not mine." He pointed out that he had requested and was granted three hours of debate on amendments when the Senate was considering his bill. His defensiveness was unusual. He didn't have his game face on.

"The majority eventually rules," he said. "I knew if we defeated the rule, we'd dramatically increase our chances. That's what Gephardt says. We're in great shape." He was vamping. It was true that the reformers were in less bad shape than they would have been if they'd lost the bill itself on the House floor. McCain said, "Now we start strategizing again. It's impossible to keep it off the floor of the House of Representatives."

McCain had put his trust in Gephardt, and he and his aides insisted that once Gephardt said that he had 190 to 195 votes for the bill but couldn't hold that many for the fourteen amendments, they had to take his word for it. If the bill, rather than the rule, failed in the House, reform would surely be dead for at least the year. Also, they didn't want Gephardt to be able to say that he could have passed the bill if only they'd helped him get a better rule.

. . .

It had been a twenty-four-hour period of quick calls and questioned judgments, but some basics seemed apparent. Gephardt wanted a bill and was working very hard to get one. McCain did a delicate diplomatic job of helping him and also holding his Senate coalition together—and of keeping key outside reformers from defecting. The Republicans opposed to reform pulled every stop—as McCain had expected. As for their spin afterwards that the reformers voted down the rule because they didn't have the votes for the bill, if that was truly the case, the opponents would have let the bill come up on the terms the reformers sought—and watch it be defeated.

Chris Shays wasn't all wrong in his assessment that Speaker Hastert would try to be fair, but, obviously, Hastert wasn't in control of his conference on this issue. McCain had been right that the trouble would come from others. The reformers gambled that they would be better off threatening to vote down the rule than letting the bill come up under conditions that might have led to no bill at all. They almost got a better rule, but the conservative Republicans—who had demanded the adverse rule in the first place—weren't going to let that happen. This overrode Gephardt's hesitation and not unreasonable request to see the mystery amendment and get some time to work on it. If the Republicans had been acting in good faith, they'd have reached a deal with Gephardt. But they didn't want to.

The whole episode left the reformers disheartened, because they had begun the week thinking that, despite the difficulties, they were going to get a bill through the House. But at least they were still alive.

The question was what to do next.

Chapter 12

"We have to find a way to force this thing."

M CCAIN HAD BEEN BUSY since the campaign finance bill was pulled from the floor of the House. Now he had a new challenge: to not let that be the end of it. He talked to Daschle about the possibility of the Senate's adding the bill to something the House wanted, and Daschle agreed. On Friday he talked to the conservative House Democrats (Blue Dogs) about starting a discharge petition, which they had successfully sponsored twice before.

He appeared on several talk shows over the weekend after the House defeated the rule and said, "I'm confident we'll have a fair vote on this." He said nice things about Hastert: "a very decent guy." "I think cooler heads are going to prevail." Asked on *Meet the Press* about his increased splitting with his party, he replied, "I have a heritage and an obligation to carry on in the tradition of Barry Goldwater and Mo Udall [the late Democratic congressman from Arizona and a close friend of McCain's], who often acted in an independent fashion." Asked if he might change parties, he said, "I am a proud Republican and I hope we can maintain the tradition of Teddy Roosevelt and Barry Goldwater."

• • •

Two days later, McCain met with House Republican reformers to discuss how they should proceed. Lindsey Graham had suggested that, given the sensitivity of the situation, McCain shouldn't begin with Gephardt. The consensus was that the best option was to go ahead with a discharge petition. Trying to attach the campaign finance bill to another bill in the Senate could pose difficulties if the Senate Republican leadership, as was to be expected, fought it. But Shays argued that before the discharge procedure was to be started, someone should go to Hastert to give him notice. McCain and the others agreed but didn't think anything would come of it.

After the meeting with the House Republican moderates, McCain called Gephardt and said that a delegation, which included Shays and Lindsey Graham, would go to Hastert to say that if he didn't schedule the bill, there'd be a petition. McCain was more convinced than ever that Hastert couldn't act on his own.

"Can you hold your people?" McCain asked Gephardt.

"I think I can."

The objective was to make a show of strength right away, and eventually convince, or force, the Republican leaders to let the bill come up again.

Speaker Hastert, as expected, declined to reschedule the bill. He said that his caucus wasn't ready for the bill to come up again, that 80 percent of it was against accommodating the reformers. In effect, he told the reform Republicans, they were going to have to force him to do it.

The following afternoon, McCain, Feingold, Daschle, Gephardt, Meehan, and some House reform Republicans met in the Capitol basement and formally decided that the discharge petition was the best way to proceed. The hope was to get the bill brought back up in September, but time was short: Because of the rules, it couldn't be signed for seven legislative days after it was filed, and there are only two Mondays a month when a discharge petition can be considered; the August recess was scheduled to begin in two weeks. Thursday afternoon, the Blue Dogs held a press conference to announce that they would file a discharge petition. McCain, Gephardt, Feingold, and Meehan attended, but Shays did not. The cover story was that Shays was attending a committee meeting, but in fact he and McCain had just had a blow-up on the phone.

Shays had called McCain to say that he didn't think McCain or Gephardt should be at the Blue Dogs' press conference and that he himself was planning to stay away. He thought that this should be simply a Blue Dogs event—that showing Gephardt and McCain as behind the petition might discourage some Republicans from sign-ing it. Their presence at the press conference had already been announced, but Shays's nerves were frayed, and he felt that he was being manipulated by McCain and Gephardt. He was still upset that his judgment had been questioned on the subject of the rule and that his strength had been found lacking, and he thought he had a real point about how best to get the most signatures on the petition.

McCain's frustration with Shays spilled over. You wanted to deal with those guys diplomatically, McCain said in effect, and we got screwed. He let Shays know that he didn't care whether or not he attended the press conference.

Jim Turner, of Texas, the head of the Blue Dogs' campaign finance task force, announced that the group had filed a discharge petition, which contained a "very fair" rule.

Turner called on McCain, who said, "No. I'm fine. Thank you." He smiled quickly. "I'm fine." He was being careful about being seen as too intrusive in the House proceedings. It's a line he'd walked with difficulty for the past couple of months: charging in when he thought he had to—and had been asked to—and standing back at other moments. But he had no intention of abdicating his role as the moral authority on this issue, or of giving up. No one else could play his particular role.

After the press conference, McCain told Meehan, "We have to find a way to force this thing. The problem is how, now that we're facing the August break." McCain was more concerned than he let on that Congress would recess for August without a campaign finance reform bill or any assurance that it would be coming back up in the fall.

A number of groups had already begun to plan an effort at persuasion: Common Cause, Wertheimer of Democracy 21, the League of Women Voters, the AARP, environmental groups, the Committee for Economic Development, Campaign for America (a group headed by the investment banker Jerome Kohlberg), and Americans for Reform (the group McCain had put together). They would make calls and take ads in the districts of people who hadn't signed the petition but who might be persuaded to. (This was later postponed on the theory that no one is home, or wants to listen to this kind of thing, in August.)

Back in his office, McCain was asked if he thought there was still a real shot at getting a bill.

"Everyone I talk to is confident that we have enough votes to win," he replied. "If we didn't have the votes to win, we'd have had a vote last week. If they had the votes, we'd have had a vote."

He rejected the suggestion that after the rule went down and it was clear there'd be no further action on the bill for some time, he'd looked glum in public for the first time during his long push for the bill.

"Throughout this whole exercise I never get excited nor

depressed. I just continue on until the day it's signed by the President, and then I'll express some emotion. I wasn't happy, but I wasn't surprised."

Buse came into the office to talk to McCain about his effort to block a Democratic amendment that would delay opening the border with Mexico to Mexican trucks, under the North American Free Trade Agreement (NAFTA), for at least another two years. McCain got into the issue because he's a strong believer in free trade, because Mexico borders on Arizona, and because he has a principled objection to putting such legislation on an appropriations bill. He thinks this only increases the appropriators' already outsized power. McCain was heavily outnumbered on the issue, but he doesn't mind fighting when he thinks a principle is involved.

The Democrats argued that the issue was safety, while opponents pointed out that the Teamsters were behind the Democrats on this matter. McCain's position put him on the side of the administration, which he didn't mind at all. He looks for such opportunities. Moreover, the co-sponsor of his effort was Phil Gramm, his supposed nemesis.

Chapter 13

"Political capital is to be spent."

S IX DAYS after the press conference on the discharge petition, McCain, in his office, cheerfully announced, "I'm in another fight at the moment."

That made three: the campaign finance bill, Mexican trucks, and now a dispute with the Democrats on the Commerce Committee (of which he used to be chairman) over their attempt to block the President's nominee to head the Consumer Products Safety Commission.

"We're having fun," he said.

The "fun," he said, "is what it's all about. Trying to get done what you think's good for the country. No sense in being unhappy about it."

Buse came in to brief him on where the Mexican trucks issue stood, and Trent Lott, of all people, called him to talk about it. They had a friendly conversation, going through names of people who might be helpful on the issue. McCain was far from the isolated figure of Washington political lore. In fact, other senators were increasingly asking him to co-sponsor their legislation.

. . .

Asked how the various issues he'd taken on have affected his standing with his conservative base, about which he was still concerned, McCain said, "Clearly you lose some of it but I lost a lot of that in the Presidential campaign. When Rush Limbaugh's tearing into you every day it's going to cause some erosion. As far as my state is concerned, I remain the most popular politician in Arizona. You hate to lose people, but you have to do what's right and realize when you get involved in certain high-visibility issues it has a certain polarizing effect."

Asked if his constituency was changing, McCain replied, "That depends on the issue. Push for more defense, that's a conservative issue. I was for school vouchers, that's a conservative issue. Campaign finance reform and the patients' bill of rights are different. So it kind of shifts around. You have to understand that sometimes you're going to have people not support you if you take certain stands. But political capital is to be spent."

That evening, McCain and Salter dropped by a fundraiser held by the Main Street Partnership, the group of Republican House moderates. Some moderates were wobbly about signing the discharge petition—confronting their leadership once again. Several of them tend to calibrate how much they want to offend their leaders. And they were under terrific and fairly constant pressure from the leaders, who do have the power to punish.

The fact that some of the moderates were rebelling against the administration's more restrictive version of the patients' bill of rights was causing some of them to say that they'd have to get to the discharge petition later. Some others were saying that they wanted to go to Hastert first and ask him to schedule the campaign finance bill—which would seem pretty futile—before they signed the petition. Some had the idea of signing in waves and then going to Hastert and asking him to schedule the bill—which was also a useless notion. John Weaver, McCain's political adviser, got so anxious when he heard about these schemes that he interrupted a vacation to come back to Washington.

At the reception, Fred Upton, Republican of Michigan, approached McCain and suggested that he make some changes in the bill. This invitation to further chaos took McCain aback, but he calmly nodded and said, "Okay, Fred, okay. We'll talk about it." He told Salter to have somebody talk to Upton, but nothing further came of it.

Meanwhile, McCain, Shays, Graham, Gephardt, and Meehan were organizing to get as many signatures as possible on the petition in the course of the following week—the last week before the August recess. The point was to put on as strong a show as they could to impress the Republican leaders, who were dubious that the petition would succeed, other House members who should sign it, and the public. They figured that when the petitions reached a certain number short of 218, Hastert would have to decide whether to schedule the bill so as to keep control of the floor. (Otherwise the House would proceed according to the rule set out in the petition.) Past Speakers had done that, but Hastert was obviously in a difficult position with his caucus and his fellow leaders.

Chapter 14

"So do me a favor and pray over it, will you, my friend?"

AT MIDMORNING on Tuesday, McCain raced into Mark Salter's office following a meeting on the House side with administration officials and Senate and House sponsors of the more far-reaching patients' bill of rights legislation that the Senate had passed and that the administration opposed. He was part of an effort to work out a compromise.

"Someone said, 'Why don't we say we had a constructive meeting. It'll move the process,' " McCain told Salter. "I said, 'We have two hundred meetings. Why don't we say what happened?' I said, 'Let's have someone from the White House say there is a deal, there isn't a deal. I'll call the President myself if necessary.' " (There wasn't a deal.)

And then they turned to the most pressing business: getting signatures for the discharge petition.

Salter told him, "We've got 157 Democrats signed yesterday, including Martin Frost." Frost, a former chairman of the Democratic

Congressional Campaign Committee, had been understood to be (like his former Senate counterpart Robert Torricelli) working against the reform bill.

That was indeed a lot of signatures in one day; the day before was the first that anyone could sign the petition. In 1998, it took six months to get 204 signatures, at which point then-Speaker Gingrich agreed to schedule the bill. The effort was being coordinated among a group consisting of Wertheimer, officials of Common Cause, Trevor Potter, Salter, Rick Davis, and Campaign for America, Kohlberg's group. Wertheimer kept the master list of who had signed and who was targeted as someone who should sign, and updated it twice a day.

McCain, Salter, and Buse move into McCain's office, and McCain sits behind his desk to make calls on the discharge petition.

Salter hands him a list of people to call. The loose coalition of people gathering the signatures has decided where McCain might have the most impact.

McCain, dialing the number himself, calls one of the Republicans on the list. "John McCain. I'd appreciate it if you'd sign the discharge petition." McCain speaks in a normal voice and doesn't press; he's simply straightforward about his request. Salter stands close by, holding a copy of the list and watching intently. "The deal is I think we can get 218 if we get a few more Republicans to sign now."

"I really appreciate it. You've been a great soldier. Once more into the breach."

He hangs up. "OK?" Salter asks. McCain nods.

McCain calls another Republican. "John McCain again. I think if we can get nine more people we can get this thing done." Pause.

"Thank you, my friend."

"He's signing?" Salter asks.

"He signed," McCain replies.

Of another Republican, McCain says, "Lindsey's the one that's gotta talk to him."

McCain calls another moderate Republican.

"Senator McCain here. We're doing OK. We need eight more signatures. If you could sign I'd really appreciate it, my friend." He mentions another Republican who's signed.

After listening to the congressman, McCain says, "Thanks. It's always good to hear from you, my friend. I'm glad you're giving it serious consideration." McCain knows that he can ask, and that his asking might have some effect, but that he can't press. A member of Congress will make up his or her own mind on such a sensitive question.

McCain tells Salter, "He's working his way through this."

"We'll get him?" Salter asks.

"We'll get him."

Salter paces. He's perturbed that some others in the coalition aren't shooting for the necessary 218 signatures this week. Some Republicans have said that they wouldn't sign until after the recess—maybe they wouldn't be needed, maybe things will have cooled down, maybe they can plead constituent pressure to sign. And some House leaders are calling for disciplining moderate Republicans who have broken with the leadership on the rule and the patients' bill of rights. So some moderates would just as soon avoid the line of fire just now.

"I promise you this is the last time I'll bug you," McCain says to a congresswoman. "It was great to see you at the Main Street event. I need you to sign the discharge petition. I love you," he says, smiling into the phone. The congresswoman has a beef about something that just happened on another piece of legislation that McCain is involved in. He listens, says, "Bless you, I understand and I appreciate that." He offers to send her some material about the issues in the legislation she's concerned about. He speaks calmly, in a low voice. "I fully understand your frustration."

After he hangs up, Salter, single-minded at this point, asks, "What about c.f.r.?"

"She's not going to do it," McCain replies.

"She's not going to do it?" Salter asks incredulously.

"She's not going to do it until she gets her other issue," McCain replies. (McCain was pleasantly surprised later that day when Salter told him the congresswoman had signed.)

He calls another moderate who has gone wobbly.

"Hey," he says, addressing the congressman, "how you doin'? They tell me if we can get eight more signatures we can get 218. The Dems say they can get over 200."

Salter quietly corrects him, "200."

McCain goes on, "So do me a favor and pray over it, will you, my friend?" And after a brief silence he thanks him.

"He's never signed a discharge petition but he'll look at it. We should get Lindsey to follow up," he tells Salter.

Another congressman tells McCain he isn't going to sign the petition.

"I understand," McCain says. "You don't have to explain it to me."

McCain says to Salter, "He's not going to do it."

"Period?" Salter asks.

"Period. I didn't ask him why."

McCain calls Lindsey Graham and greets him in a deep, gravelly voice that he sometimes jokily uses, and then says, "I'm just missing my time at Bob Jones University." (Bush famously visited the controversial school during the South Carolina primary; McCain did not.) Then he tells Graham which House Republicans he thinks Graham should talk to or Shays should talk to. (There's no direct communication between Shays and McCain at this point.)

Citizen McCain

·   ·   ·

McCain is buzzed and told that New York Governor George Pataki is calling him. McCain is surprised. He and Pataki, a strong Bush supporter in 2000, had had a collision over New York's rules, which would have kept McCain electors off the ballot. McCain held a press conference in front of the Russian consulate in New York—saying there was now more democracy in Russia than in the New York Republican Party—and got on the ballot.

McCain greets Pataki in a friendly way and jokes, "We're trying to get those Mexican trucks all the way to New York."

After listening for a while, McCain says excitedly, "I'd be honored. It would be one of the great thrills of my life."

After McCain hangs up, he says, still excited, "The hundredth anniversary of Teddy Roosevelt. Big ceremony at Sagamore Hill." (Roosevelt became President on September 14, 1901, after the assassination of William McKinley. Sagamore Hill was the home that Roosevelt built in Oyster Bay.) "I'm really fired up."

Then he jumps up from behind his desk, scoots over to the chair where he'd slung his fat, battered briefcase, pulls out a book, and starts reading a quote of Roosevelt from it (*T.R.: The Last Romantic,* by H. W. Brands). " 'All of us who give service, and stand ready for sacrifice, are the torch-bearers.' "

"That's my boy!"

And he continues, " 'We run with the torches until we fall, content if we can pass them to the hands of other runners. These are the torch-bearers; these are they who have dared the Great Adventure.' "

Chapter 15

"The more you do the more you do."

T HE HOUSE was to begin its recess on Thursday, and perhaps the Senate as well, and McCain had many matters on his hands. The previous evening, the White House preempted the patients' bill of rights negotiations by luring Representative Charlie Norwood, a dentist and Republican from Georgia, and heretofore one of the sponsors of the stronger legislation, into a meeting with Bush and forcing upon him a compromise. Norwood wasn't allowed to confer with his co-sponsors or even to leave the White House until the President appeared with him in the press room announcing that an agreement had been reached.

Other sponsors of the legislation were highly perturbed and scrambling to find out what was in the White House "deal." McCain told the *New York Times* that it "favors the H.M.O. over the patient," which worried Salter, because their strategy was that McCain be one of the brokers when the Senate and House bills went to conference. McCain's role was to be John the Statesman, with his office answering press queries by saying that they were still studying the compromise. He had slipped with the *Times* because it's hard for him not to say what he thinks. (He received a staff report that there were prob-

lems with the compromise but that they could be fixed in conference.) Difficult as it was for him to remain mum, he had a larger goal
in mind, which was to end the five-year-long stalemate on the issue.

McCain and Gramm decided to give up for the time being their
delaying tactics against the legislation on Mexican trucks, so as not to
be seen as holding up the recess—this was a nod to reality.

McCain continued to make phone calls to House Republicans
on the discharge petition. A couple of people told him that they
would sign after the recess—possibly in the hope that such an act of
courage wouldn't be necessary. The counters and keepers of the list
said that some Democrats and Republicans hadn't signed but should,
based on their past support of campaign reform—enough, in fact, to
have the petition succeed in September. Also in September, the outside game would recommence. McCain was planning some events
outside of Washington. The phone calls from outside groups would
intensify. The immediate goal was to get as many signatures as possible before the House went home for August.

In the midst of all this, McCain kept a commitment on Thursday
morning he had made a few weeks before to Lawrence Eagleburger, the
former Secretary of State and a friend, to appear at a rally at the Capitol for some Israeli POWs believed to be held by Hezbollah forces in
Lebanon. (Eagleburger was blocked by the White House from becoming a member of the prestigious President's Foreign Intelligence Advi-
sory Board, apparently because he supported McCain in 2000.)

About forty people, including Eagleburger and the Israeli ambas-
sador, and the leader of the World Jewish Congress, waited for
McCain in his office while he attended a self-congratulation ceremony held by the President in the House chamber. Bush had succeeded in getting his energy legislation and his compromise of the

patients' bill of rights through the House. McCain returned to his office, greeted the visiting delegation as if he had nothing else to do, and headed with it to "the swamp," a paved-over area just outside the Russell Building, where press conferences are sometimes held under a large oak tree. A large number of television cameras had assembled. McCain said, "We're honored to have with us the Speaker of the Knesset," and he referred to four Israeli soldiers, "in service of their country made captive by terrorist forces." Referring to the captives' families who were present, he said, "I always felt, when I was in captivity in Hanoi, that it was more difficult for my family than for me."

McCain stood patiently while various members of the captives' families and Israeli officials spoke, though he had much to do, and he didn't dash away when it was over.

A reporter from Televisa, Mexican television, wanted to know about the Mexican trucks. McCain's opposition to the amendment delaying their entry into the country had fanned the issue—not accidentally—into a big story in the American papers. McCain replied, "It's obvious it's the Teamsters Union that's a major factor."

Then he raced over to the Senate floor to present an amendment about the formula allocating water to the various states, which he argued hadn't been changed to reflect Arizona's rapid growth in population. The previous Sunday, he had flown to Arizona (he'd been attending his son Jack's graduation from the Sea Cadets summer camp program at Fort Dix, New Jersey) to hold a hearing on the heated issue there of where to build a new football stadium—in Tempe or Phoenix. Despite his national prominence, he wasn't ignoring his home state.

• • •

On the way back to his office, I commented to McCain on how much he seemed to have going on. He had started early in the morning with a 7:25 appearance on Don Imus's show; he got into a fracas with Democrats on the Commerce Committee over their blocking the President's appointment to head the Consumer Products Safety Commission.

"Yep, yep," McCain replied, "I'm still going to make some calls on the discharge petition. But the House is going out tonight. I've found that the more you do, the more you do—you just crowd it in."

McCain was scheduled to begin a vacation that weekend with his family on Lake Powell, in northern Arizona, and then take a raft trip with them down the Colorado River. After that, he was to take a five-day trip to Latvia, Bulgaria, the Czech Republic, and Estonia—on the subject of NATO enlargement, which he favors. And then back to Washington after Labor Day, to go at the discharge petition and everything else on his plate again.

As McCain enters the outer door that leads to Mark Salter's office, he calls out, "Mark, Mark," and Salter and Buse materialize and go into his office with him.

Salter, talking about the discharge petition, suggests McCain call Mark Foley, a Florida Republican, who had voted before for the Shays-Meehan bill.

"I did that yesterday," McCain says.

Salter suggests Charles Bass, of New Hampshire, for whom McCain campaigned in 2000.

"I talked to him at the President's event," McCain replies.

Salter asks, "What did he say?"

"He's not going to do it," McCain replies.

"Not until after the recess?"

"Not going to do it," McCain says. "Maybe need more pressure on him." (Bass did sign later.) And then he volunteers that he talked to Rodney Frelinghuysen, a moderate from New Jersey, when he was at the President's celebration.

"I'll put in another call to Foley, if you want," McCain offers, "but I'd like a sandwich."

Salter, not dropping a stitch, says that if Frelinghuysen signs, "that should open up other people."

McCain's staff anticipated he'd want a sandwich, so Ives brings a salami sub. Looking sad, McCain says, "I apologize, but I've had a hundred and twenty-seven of them in a row. How about a BLT?"

"Okay," Ives replies, cheerful as always.

"Thank you very much and God bless you," McCain says.

Rick Davis has joined the group as they discuss the tone McCain should take in talking about the patients' bill of rights compromise: The emphasis is that he should say "progress has been made," and there are issues that "need to be worked on in conference."

Salter reports that a veteran of their 2000 New Hampshire campaign wants to hold a reunion and has asked if McCain could make an appearance. Given the sensitivities and suspicions surrounding McCain's intentions, this is, of course, not a good idea. Salter says, "I said right off the top that I think if John went up there it would be misunderstood."

Salter, still focused on the petition, asks McCain if he saw Jim Ramstad, of Minnesota, when he was over in the House chamber.

"He told me he was going to sign," McCain says.

"But he hasn't," Salter replies. "It would be a good idea to break two hundred before the House goes out tonight."

McCain says, "It might be a good idea for you to call him and say, 'Hey, you told McCain you'd sign and he's willing to do something with you in Minnesota.' " Salter says McCain is already planning to be in Minnesota in the fall and goes off to make the call. Shortly, Salter returns to report that Ramstad will sign but wants to tell McCain himself. (Ramstad did sign before the recess.)

They talk about a possible September event in Swarthmore, Pennsylvania, to drum up support for the discharge petition. McCain wonders why that's so important and is told that a major backer of reform has ties there and wants an event there.

"OK," McCain replies reluctantly. "But you've got to balance being home as well as doing this."

Salter tells him he can do the event on a Monday.

"Okay, what else?"

Salter reports that there's nothing new in Arizona. They're keeping an eye on what might be happening back home. The recall petition is still alive.

Asked what happens if he doesn't get the necessary signatures, McCain replies, "I don't have any thinking about what we do if we don't get it. I'm devoting all my efforts toward that. We got the Senate vote and we beat an unfair rule, and you just keep plugging along."

By Thursday night, the discharge petition had 205 signatures. Only thirteen more would be needed to get the bill back before the House in the fall. Even some congenital pessimists were becoming optimistic that the House would pass the bill in the fall.

McCain didn't get out of Washington until Friday. Before he did, he instructed Mark Buse to put in the Congressional Record a colloquy between himself and Joe Lieberman that proposed a plan for the United States to reduce greenhouse gases. McCain, who had held hearings on global warming and was convinced it was a problem, was the first Senate Republican to call for such action. "The current situation demands leadership from the United States," he said. The administration, which was in political difficulty over the global-warming issue for having pulled out of the Kyoto Protocol without having yet participated in negotiations on an alternative pact, wasn't likely to appreciate McCain's parting gift.

Chapter 16

"They are acts of war."

JOHN MCCAIN returned to Washington on Tuesday, September 4, when the Senate reconvened following the August recess, expecting a relatively quiet period and relaxed (for him) schedule. He needed the slower pace because six days earlier he had undergone surgery for a benign enlargement of the prostate. Some of his advisers had argued that he should postpone his return for a week, but McCain, not one for accepting physical limits, wouldn't buy that. Besides, he and his wife wanted to go to the Bushes' first state dinner, for Mexican President Vicente Fox, on September 5. Still, several events that had been planned for McCain were cancelled.

McCain was planning to make a few phone calls to get more signatures for the discharge petition. The House would be in session for only about ten days in September, largely because of the Jewish holidays in addition to their usual long weekends, and the easier signatures had already been obtained. The reformers expected to gather enough to bring the bill back to the House floor in October. Just before he left Phoenix, McCain received a call from Gephardt saying that he would be getting signatures one at a time now, and that it would be difficult, but that he could get enough.

Pale-faced and moving slowly, McCain cast a vote late Tuesday afternoon and went home. The next day he made calls on the discharge petition, which gained two more signatures—for 207 out of the needed 218—over the next couple of days. Another member, Richard Neal of Massachusetts, said that though he never signed discharge petitions, he would be willing to be the 218th to sign.

McCain also held a press conference with Shays, Meehan, and Feingold to urge other House members to sign the petition. ("No one believes that someone who pays hundreds of thousands of dollars for a fundraiser is interested in good government," McCain said.) He attended a couple of committee meetings; discussed with staff the status of other legislation; issued a statement on his bill, co-sponsored with Chuck Schumer, to make generic drugs more available; and lunched with Cindy and his eighty-nine-year-old, straight-backed and hearty mother, Roberta, who lives in Washington, and on Friday with Warren Beatty, Annette Bening, and their children.

At the White House dinner, McCain told the President that he wouldn't be able to stay for the entertainment after the dinner because of his recent surgery, but he enjoyed himself. McCain was seated at Laura Bush's table, where Fox was also seated, and Cindy was seated at a table with Colin Powell, also prime seating.

The following Monday, the discharge petition received two more signatures, for a total of 210, counting Neal. Greg Ganske, Republican of Iowa, said that he would sign once he found out if he was appointed a conferee on the patients' bill of rights. (He would sign the petition either way but, as a proponent of the stronger bill, was holding off so that he might be appointed, which wasn't likely.) That meant that the reformers needed only seven more signatures, which they were confident that they could get over the next couple of weeks. That afternoon, after debate among his staff over whether he should go, McCain kept an appointment to fly to Boston to receive, along with John Kerry, of Massachusetts, also a Vietnam veteran, an award from the World Affairs Council for their work on normalizing relations with Vietnam.

Citizen McCain

. . .

On Tuesday morning, September 11, McCain drove to his office later than usual because he hadn't returned from Boston until past midnight the night before. (Unlike many senators, McCain refuses to be chauffeured.) Shortly after his car crossed the 14th Street bridge into Washington, he heard the news on the radio that a plane had slammed into one of the towers of the World Trade Center. When he reached Capitol Hill he went straight to Salter's office, where they and other staff members in the cramped office, watching the television set, saw a second plane hit the other tower. "This is war," McCain said quietly. While he and Salter were talking about what to do, whether they should put out a statement, Joe Donohue, his personal assistant, came and told them that the Pentagon had just been hit by a plane.

Suddenly, there was the sound of two loud explosions. Radio reports suggested, erroneously, that the State Department had been bombed, that the Capitol had been bombed. (It turned out that the noise was the sound of sonic booms as jets scrambled at Andrews Air Force Base, nearby in Maryland.) As office workers became upset, Salter told them to leave—a little later they learned from watching television that the Capitol building was being evacuated.

The scene on Capitol Hill was chaotic. There was no timely warning by the Capitol police to evacuate. There was no evacuation plan for the elected politicians and their numerous aides—thousands of people. There was no plan for evacuating the Supreme Court. (There was a plan for spiriting away the congressional leadership, who were sent to an undisclosed place, where they spent more time with each other than they had all year.)

Before McCain and Salter left the office, Ives issued the statement they'd decided on: "There are no words to describe adequately the enormity of these attacks on the United States or the depravity of those who are responsible for them. . . . These were not just crimes against the United States, they are acts of war. We will prevail in this war, as we have prevailed in the past." And then they got in their cars and were quickly trapped in the gridlock surrounding Capitol Hill. Given the lack of planning, if the plane that went down in Pennsylvania that morning after some passengers courageously took on the hijackers had in fact been headed for Capitol Hill, the result could have been catastrophic.

McCain got as far as one block in thirty minutes. "This will take forever," he complained. Donohue told him that one of the staff members, Sonya Sotak, McCain's legislative assistant for health policy and other domestic issues, had said that she lived on Capitol Hill and that they could come to her apartment if traffic became too difficult. At the time and for much of the rest of the day, the cell-phone system was overloaded, and it was nearly impossible to make outgoing calls, but Donohue managed to get through on McCain's phone to Salter, also stuck in the traffic, and suggested that they meet at Sotak's apartment. While there, Salter received calls from numerous news organizations and anchors or producers, asking for comments by McCain.

Over the next few days, McCain's was to become the most sought-after voice in Washington, and he offered more leadership then than did the President. On the Tuesday of the attacks, Bush had hopscotched from air force base to air force base. (The White House put out an explanation that this was because the President's mansion was an intended target of the plane that went into the Pentagon, or that Air Force One was a target—this explanation was later backed off from.) What statements the President did make seemed unsure. He was still finding his voice on the matter.

"The best thing that we can do as Americans is to remain calm," McCain told ABC. "Obviously, this is an act of war that has been committed against the United States," he told another interviewer.

He phoned his wife a couple of times to assure her that he was all right. He became upset when he learned that the schools in Phoenix had been closed. "My God, they're panicking," he said, and so in most of his calls he told people not to panic, that the President would return to Washington, that the government was functioning, and that people were secure.

Later that afternoon, McCain, Salter, and Donohue repaired to Salter's house in Alexandria, where Ives was to join them. Salter thought they should all be in one place to coordinate the press requests. McCain also initiated calls to numerous Arizona radio and television stations to urge calm.

Finally, at 7:00 P.M., after talking to seventeen Arizona and national media, a fatigued McCain went home to his apartment in northern Virginia.

Chapter 17

"This is going to be a long twilight struggle."

O N WEDNESDAY MORNING, McCain came into the office early to appear on morning television programs—ABC, CBS, and *Imus in the Morning*—and to catch up on paperwork and to do his ritual reading of the morning papers.

On the morning programs, he began to say that the fight against terrorism "will be a long struggle," that the United States was up against "a veritable network [of terrorism] in that part of the world." He was beginning to try to prepare the American people for a new kind of struggle and to persuade them to be patient. "Just launching a bunch of cruise missiles, so-called pinprick responses, that we employed before is not going to do it, and everybody knows that."

During the 2000 campaign, McCain had frequently called the Clinton administration's response to terrorist attacks "a feckless photo-op foreign policy, for which we may pay a heavy price in American blood and treasure." He had also said frequently, "We've known for a long time that terrorist groups are not only planning but also have committed attacks against the United States." He had warned then that the rise of radical Islamic fundamentalism and the fact that terrorist groups were trying to develop weapons of mass destruction were threats to the United States.

And now, in his radio and television interviews, he was trying to prepare the public for the consequences of the latest terror attack: "It's going to take a lot of work, a lot of effort, a lot of American treasure and perhaps some American blood."

Shortly before ten, McCain's talking by phone to Channel 10 in Phoenix. Salter is with him, listening and reading the papers. McCain praises the President's statement of the previous evening after he returned to Washington. Though Bush began, in his brief address from the White House, to rally the nation, to lay out the terms of the issue—"We will make no distinction between the terrorists who committed these acts and those who harbor them"—his delivery was hasty and nervous. But McCain knows that, whatever his own misgivings about the leadership the President is offering right now, or about the President, he must be supported publicly; the nation must be held together at this moment.

"Ron," McCain says in the phone interview, "first of all the message from America is that we're coming after you," and he points out, "There is a broad variety of responses that can be deployed and deployed quickly—cruise missiles, ground troops, special forces operations will take longer." He adds, "We're in this for the long haul."

Then he talks to another Phoenix television station. "We have to make it clear this is an act of war and discourage other acts of war."

When he finishes his several calls, I ask McCain what the effect of the recent events would have on the broad range of issues he'd been working on. "This knocked everything into a cocked hat," he replies. "It's just a higher priority than everything else." He glances at the television set and remarks, "The Pentagon's still burning." As the ranking member of the Commerce Committee, he will be involved in issues of airline safety, he says, and as a member of the Armed Services Committee he'll be addressing a number of issues that the recent events have raised.

McCain has been quick to see that the terrorist attack is a transforming event, and he's now as focused on that as he had been, up until two days before, on other issues of great importance to him. "We just have to put everything on hold until we get this situation in hand. It's an overwhelming event. It's an historic event. We can't turn our focus away from it. The United States has just had an act of war committed on it. It's a transcendent event. It supersedes everything else." Then he goes over to the Capitol.

As he nears the Senate floor, a reporter asks him about the President. "He's doing a marvelous job," McCain replies.

"What's next?" the reporter asks. McCain replies, "We'll break their backs. We'll do whatever is necessary to break their backs—put them out of business." He says, "No country that engages in this kind of thing will be free from pressure—diplomatic, economic, military."

This isn't an unfamiliar role for McCain, except that his voice and leadership are more in demand than ever before. Nor is it the first time that he has put aside matters of importance to him in the interest of meeting what he feels is a foreign policy demand. In 1999 he acted as a prod to the Clinton administration to get involved in Kosovo, and, once the bombing started, he put off a planned six-city tour to announce his presidential candidacy—which among other things cost the campaign some of its funds (it's expensive simply to lay on such a tour), which at that point weren't plentiful. This time, at this point, McCain doesn't feel he has to act as a prod to the Bush administration, but he knows that people will listen to him. His role, as he sees it, is to prepare public opinion for what he feels has to come.

It's an eerie day on Capitol Hill—quiet, subdued. No tourists are around; the police have made the place inaccessible to anyone without a special pass and diverted traffic several blocks away. Inside the Capitol, the souvenir stand and the tourists' dining room are shut down.

As the two parties break from their weekly lunches, there is another sense of how much things have changed. A Democratic senator says that Carl Levin, chairman of the Armed Services Committee, who had recently gotten his committee to scale back the administration's request for a missile defense program, told his colleagues he thought the issue should be put off in the interest of national unity. Kent Conrad, of North Dakota and chairman of the Budget Committee, who had been making a big fuss about the administration's dipping into funds supposedly set aside for Social Security (as a result of its large tax-cut bill), tells reporters, "There is no question that we are behind finding the resources to defend the country and rebuild. Our top priority is to defend the nation. The protection of the trust funds is also a priority, and we'll deal with that over time. Everything has changed. We've been attacked. We are at war."

At 3:45 McCain gives his speech on the Senate floor. It's a strong one, in which he says that the attacks "have aroused in this great nation a controlled fury and unity of purpose not just to punish but to vanquish our enemies." He continues, "I say to our enemies, we are coming. God may show you mercy. We will not."

And then he gives a live interview to Tom Brokaw from the Russell Building Rotunda.

"The President is working hard," McCain tells Brokaw, "as well as Colin Powell and Condoleezza Rice [the President's national security adviser]."

He's asked about the mood on Capitol Hill.

"I think it's changed, and I think the change is genuine. How long that will last is anybody's guess."

In a live interview with Bob Schieffer, of CBS, a few minutes later, McCain says, "I think it's going to be a long struggle."

He's being a leader, defining the terms of the situation and trying to prepare the public. His style on television, calm, low-key, and direct, helps him make his case and makes people more willing to listen to him than they are to the posturers and self-dramatists.

That evening, on CNN, McCain took his case a step further by saying, "It wouldn't be over if we got rid of Mr. Bin Laden tomorrow. There are other organizations that are bent on the destruction of the United States."

The next morning, Thursday, McCain was back on NBC, saying, "This has to be a sustained effort."

On Thursday afternoon McCain is in the Russell Building Rotunda again, giving an interview to Ron Insana, of CNBC. Now he's using new terminology to make his point. He says, "This is going to be a long twilight struggle"—a phrase from John F. Kennedy's Inaugural Address. "If there's anything Americans should know about this, it's that it's going to be a long struggle."

Back in his office, McCain is asked about the subtext of his talk about a long struggle, because there usually is one.

He replies, "I have to say that over and over and over and over because Americans have gotten used to Grenada and the Persian Gulf—quick fixes. We haven't been involved in a long struggle since the Vietnam War."

McCain sees it as his role to communicate, console, explain the new circumstances the country is in, to help maintain unity. Nancy Ives, busier than ever fielding requests for press interviews, says, "It supersedes everything else in his world now—to get on the public airwaves and reassure and buck up the public."

In the late afternoon on Thursday, two days after the attack, McCain, still recuperating from the surgery, is fatigued and—very rare for him—he admits it. He tries to keep his energy up by eating candy bars during interviews. At 5:25, he leaves the office to go over to the Capitol to vote on an appropriations bill, and from there he's to tape an interview for *The Charlie Rose Show.* At 5:40, the Capitol is evacuated for what turned out to be a bomb scare. McCain had parked outside the Capitol, to go from there to the television studio, but the Capitol police, in another brilliant stroke, wouldn't let anyone drive away from the Capitol grounds. So McCain, concerned he would be late for the taping, and wanting to get home, postponed it.

In his television appearances over the first weekend after the attack, McCain introduced a couple of additional new elements into his message. Unable, under the circumstances, to introduce just then his national service program, McCain began to insert the idea into his response to the war on terrorism. "In my failed presidential campaign," he said on CNN, "I saw young Americans were prepared not only to serve their neighborhood, their communities, and their country, but they were eager to. And I think [now] you're going to see young Americans galvanized with a sense of duty and purpose that will equal that of the 'greatest generation.' "

He also began to talk about his concern over the "rise of anti-Middle East sentiment" in the United States. A man whom someone took to be of Middle Eastern appearance (actually, he was a Sikh) had been shot to death in Mesa, Arizona, that week. McCain said that all American leaders had to speak out against such sentiment. And he began to talk about the need to address economic, social, and political problems in the Middle East. Recalling perhaps the book on the Crusades he had read in the spring, he pointed out that the word "assassins" came from that period, that it was an Arabic term for people willing to sacrifice their own lives in battle for their cause.

Asked the next day, on *Fox News Sunday,* about what military options should be considered, McCain replied, "I do not foreclose any option. I thought the grave mistake we made in the Kosovo situation was that we said we won't send ground troops."

And then he explained the rationale behind his strong statements about going after terrorists and countries that help them: "The only way they're going to come around—let's have a little straight talk here—is if they believe their existence is threatened. . . . These people have to understand that we are serious, we're not going to back off. We're in a long, long hard struggle, and we do not intend to give up."

In a town meeting on MSNBC on Sunday night, McCain turned to another theme that he had been talking about in some of his radio interviews, justifying military action. He mentioned the bombing of the Marine barracks in Beirut in 1983, the bombing of Pan Am flight 103 over Lockerbie, Scotland, in 1988, and other terrorist actions, which "frankly, we have done very little about." And, he said, "revenge should not be our motive; our motive is to prevent this from ever happening again."

On Monday and Tuesday, with Congress out of session, McCain crisscrossed his state, making television appearances, comforting and reassuring high school students—telling them, "We will prevail"—and hugging firefighters who were about to go to New York to help out. (The recall petition was dropped on Monday.)

On Tuesday afternoon, he boarded a plane for Burbank, California. That night, a week after the attack, Jay Leno was to do his first show since then, and he had asked McCain to be his sole guest. McCain's staff had debated whether such an appearance would be appropriate and decided to go ahead after receiving assurances from Leno that it was to be a serious show, no jokes.

The appearance on *The Tonight Show* was McCain's most affecting yet. Leno's sensitive monologue set the mood, and McCain was aware of the moment and the opportunity to speak to a large national audience. Speaking without notes, in an eloquent accumulation of the themes he had been building, making them into a new whole, McCain said,

This is the greatest nation on earth. We're the strongest nation, economic and militarily. More important, we are a beacon of hope, liberty, and freedom to everybody throughout the world, including Arab countries where the majority of the people are good and decent, peace-loving people. Let's not forget that, my friends. . . . We cannot discriminate against them in this country or anyplace else. No other nation on earth would react with the nobility that this nation has reacted with; this is a sign of our strength and our greatness. What we have seen is a new chapter in the history of this country about heroes. We have heroes today who are firefighters, who are policemen, who were on a plane and decided, said over a cell phone that this is the end and we need to do what we need to do. This is a nation of heroes, and in our sorrow we can think of them with great pride. And we will prevail. We will prevail. We will prevail. . . .

We have men and women in the military that are highly trained and highly skilled. And one of the interesting and uplifting things that has happened in the last few days, more and more young men and women have gone down to volunteer, to join the armed services. It's really remarkable. . . .

What the President and what I want to tell the American people is that we have to have patience here, my friends. This is an elusive enemy. We could launch some cruise missiles tonight and watch it on CNN and see some spectacular fireworks. . . . We have tried that in the past, and it hasn't worked. . . . It's going to require planning; it's going to require patience. And remember, our motive is not revenge; our motive is to keep this from ever having to happen again. Revenge is too broad an emotion. Our goal should be never again to let American lives be threatened like this. . . .

If Mr. Bin Laden was sent to the U.S. tomorrow and brought to trial, we would still have the same problem because there are so many other terrorist organizations doing the same thing. . . .

Asked by Leno, "What can normal people do to help?" McCain replied:

Live a normal life. Their goal, their object, is to destroy the American way of life. The best way to defeat that is to not let them do that. We'll have our freedoms, we'll have our independence, we'll have our disagreements. If you were planning on traveling, travel. If you were planning on buying something, buy it. Young people, if you were thinking about joining the armed forces, think about it. Young people, volunteer in your community. There is a lot to be done now. Give blood. Do what we see all over, do what I saw from my car on the way here tonight, and what I see all over Arizona: Fly the flag. Fly it proudly.

Chapter 18

"Such a debt you incur for life."

McCAIN STILL had pressing matters back in Washington. There were legislative matters regarding the war to be dealt with. By mid-October, it was all the clearer that most other issues would be set aside for the rest of the congressional session. The growing consensus among the congressional leaders was that, under the circumstances, controversial legislation should not be brought up because now more than ever, the American people didn't want to see partisan arguing.

This meant that though the outlook for it had been promising on September 10, campaign finance reform was dead for the 2001 session of Congress. A House Democratic leadership aide said, "With a concerted effort, we could have got the signatures in a week." He added, as a testament to McCain's standing on the matter, "Whenever McCain thinks it's okay to do it, we can hit the gas." Moreover, Campaign for America, the group sponsored by Jerome Kohlberg, had quietly conducted surveys in twenty-nine congressional districts—of House members the reformers wanted to sign the discharge petition or vote for the bill—and were prepared to show balky legislators that there was strong support for reform back home. On the question of whether Speaker Dennis Hastert should allow a fair vote on the bill itself, a survey in Hastert's own very Republican Illinois district showed that more than fifty percent of *Republicans* said that he should. (These results were not released because the bill was in abeyance.)

Other legislation, such as the patients' bill of rights, was in question. Legislation mandating sped-up congressional consideration of any trade agreements the President may have reached ("fast track") was put off. The thinking on Capitol Hill as of mid-October was that Congress should pass whatever legislation was needed for the emergency, and the appropriations bills to keep the government running, and go home.

A leading House Democrat said, "The general feeling, on both sides, is we can't appear not to be cooperative. To have a contentious debate now on education, trade, missile defense could signal to the public that the institutions couldn't come together in a time of crisis."

McCain, asked why we couldn't conduct a war, especially what might be a long one, and also govern the country at the same time, replied, "That's one way to look at it. The other may be we can't fight over lesser issues while we're in a war. The American people don't want us to."

Didn't this mean that the balance of power had shifted to the administration, which could now define what was "controversial" and avoid unwanted legislation, such as campaign finance reform or the patients' bill of rights?

"All these issues pale compared to what is a threat to our nation," McCain replied. "But we will revisit them."

Meanwhile, McCain was deeply involved in legislation to help the airline industry, already ailing before the September 11 attack, then hit with a temporary shutdown after the attack, and then much lower passenger loads once flying resumed. As Commerce Committee Chairman, McCain had been fairly tough on the airlines—urging more competition—but now, as its ranking member, he was concerned that a vital national industry was in peril, and so he strongly urged—including in a phone conversation with Bush—a bailout package of grants and loan guarantees, which was passed by the House and the Senate.

McCain was instrumental in the tightening of a resolution authorizing the President to use force. McCain and John Kerry narrowed the resolution by linking it to the attacks on September 11, rather than allowing it to be a blank check. He had said on NPR that the Gulf of Tonkin resolution "taught us that we ought to be very careful what we do in the passions of the moment and we may regret later on." He helped put some controls on the $20 billion that Congress authorized for the recovery effort in New York, so that the decisions on how it would be spent wouldn't be left to the appropriations committees, whom he didn't trust not to spend it on their own parochial interests or on pork. And he would guide a bill through the Senate to provide greater airline safety by, among other things, upgrading baggage screeners by making them federal employees. This was to prove more difficult than common sense might suggest.

Meanwhile, McCain continued to use his ever-increasing standing on trying to reassure the public and also prepare it for a long struggle. In so doing, he was also trying to conduct a bit of psychological warfare on the terrorists and their hosts. Again, McCain had a subtext. "The longer we tell them it's going to take," he said on CNN, "the shorter it will be."

Asked if he was concerned that military action would provoke instability in Pakistan and other areas in the Middle East, McCain said that was "a very great concern, particularly Pakistan, which has an unelected government and a large fundamentalist population, but we have no choice; and without the cooperation of Pakistan our options are largely reduced."

He also said, "I'm consciously trying to get across an appeal to young people's patriotism." (McCain still planned to offer his national service plan before Congress went out for the year.)

For whatever reasons, the President's rhetoric was starting to resemble McCain's in certain respects. In his address to a Joint Session of Congress on Thursday night, September 20, Bush talked of the need for patience on the part of the American people and declared a "war on terror," not just on Osama bin Laden and the Taliban government of Afghanistan. As for other nations, he limited the scope somewhat by giving notice to every nation that "continues to harbor or support terrorists," and applying the policy to "every terrorist group of global reach," but still set an ambitious goal, sometimes using Churchillian prose that didn't quite fit him.

McCain was full of praise for Bush's speech. In New York the next day, at the invitation of Mayor Rudolph Giuliani, whose take-charge, calming leadership after the attacks McCain deeply admired, McCain, speaking on the mayor's weekly radio program, called Bush's speech "informative and motivating. The most important thing the President said last night was we have to have a lot of patience." In the coming days, in other appearances, McCain described Bush's speech as "magnificent."

McCain returned to Washington on Friday afternoon in order to vote that evening on the airline bailout bill, and on Saturday he flew to California on a special mission.

On the day after United Flight 93, from Newark to San Francisco, went down in Pennsylvania, the mother of Mark Bingham, one of the passengers who had decided to take on the hijackers, appeared on *Good Morning America* and said of her son, "Incidentally, he is a big supporter of Senator John McCain. We were very touched by the eloquence of Senator McCain earlier."

Later that week, Bingham's mother asked McCain to speak at the memorial service for her son in Berkeley on Saturday. For McCain, there was no question but that he would do it. So, despite his fatigue, McCain flew across the country to deliver a eulogy for Mark Bingham. There was no publicity about the event.

In his eulogy, McCain said,

I didn't know Mark Bingham. We met once briefly during my presidential campaign, yet I cannot say that I knew him well. But I wish I had. I wish I had. . . . I love my country, and I take pride in serving her. But I cannot say that I love her more or as well as Mark Bingham did, or the other heroes on United Flight 93 who gave their lives to prevent our enemies from inflicting an even greater injury on our country. . . . It is now believed that the terrorists on Flight 93 intended to crash the airplane into the United States Capitol where I work, the great house of democracy where I was that day. . . . I may very well owe my life to Mark and the others who summoned the enormous courage of love necessary to deny those depraved, hateful men their terrible triumph. Such a debt you incur for life. I will try very hard, very hard, to discharge my public duties in a manner that honors their memory. . . . To all of you who loved Mark, and were loved by him, he will never be so far from you that you cannot feel his love. As our faith informs us, you will see him again, when our loving God reunites us all with the loved ones who preceded us. Take care of each other until then, as he would want you to. May God bless Mark. And may God bless us all.

On *Face the Nation* the next day, McCain was asked about a statement by Defense Secretary Donald Rumsfeld, who preceded him on the program. Rumsfeld had suggested that the U.S. might use nuclear arms: "The United States, to my knowledge, has never ruled out the . . . first use of nuclear weapons."

McCain replied that he thought "it's not necessary. We have . . . precision weapons and of the kind that would probably address this kind of threat, which is specific small groups of people in remote places, without having to use nuclear weapons. And very frankly, nuclear weapons have a connotation associated with them that, it seems to me, if you can't rule it out you should certainly say that it is highly unlikely that this requirement would ever arise."

Asked whether it was beyond the capabilities of the United States to combat terrorism, McCain said, "I'm absolutely convinced that it's in the capabilities of this country."

Chapter 19

"The White House has been captured
by the House leaders."

"THANKS, Gary, good to be with you." Pause. "Oh, yes, I think he's leading the country in a very fine fashion."

On Thursday afternoon, October 4, McCain is standing at his desk giving an interview by telephone to a Tucson radio station.

"I think the point is when the Russians left Afghanistan we didn't pay attention, and they developed a Pol Pot–type government.

"You have to remember, Gary, that this Northern Alliance is a very disparate group, and after they win, we have to get them to work together and with others and you don't have a bunch of warlords and corrupt people.

"The Saudis are shaky. The Saudis have serious domestic problems. Others in the coalition are doing okay, and the pleasant surprise is the Russians.

"I'm pleased at the way things are going and the President is doing a great job and I have a lot of confidence in Colin Powell and Cheney and Rumsfeld. The Congress is very united behind the President."

McCain then talks about the possible roles of Uzbekistan, Tajikistan, Turkmenistan, countries on the northern border of Afghanistan.

"Thanks, Gary."

He hangs up the phone, shrugs, and says, "Beats me."

This is the John McCain who can't take himself too seriously. He's given now over a hundred interviews in the past three weeks and he's dead serious about the purpose of his role as a national spokesman and soother, but he's taking a break from solemnity. In fact, McCain is well informed about the war on terrorism; some administration officials quietly keep him abreast of what's going on.

He had spent much of the morning in shuttle negotiations between Lott's office and Daschle's office, to try to get unstuck a bill to provide for more safety on airlines. The bill, sponsored by himself and Fritz Hollings, Democrat of South Carolina and now chairman of the Commerce Committee, contained several provisions, including strengthening cockpit doors and providing more secure perimeters of airports. But the one that was causing other Republicans to hold it up would make baggage screeners at the nation's 142 largest airports federal employees, subject to higher standards than the current low-wage, highly transient, workers hired by the airlines. Though this proposal appeared to have majorities in both Houses of Congress, the most conservative members of the House Republican leadership objected to adding twenty-eight thousand employees to the rolls of the federal government, and some of their Senate counterparts agreed.

Another problem was that Democrats were trying to add extra unemployment help for laid-off workers. In order to get the airline safety bill through quickly, McCain thought help for the laid-off workers should be included in a separate bill to stimulate the economy. Republicans were opposed to the extra benefits and so were preventing Senate debate on the bill.

In fact, both party caucuses in both chambers were becoming restive under the bipartisanship that was supposed to reign during this post-attack period and were putting pressure on their leaders.

House and Senate Democrats alike thought that their leaders were yielding too much to the White House and were angry that help for laid-off airline workers hadn't been included in the bill to bail out the airlines. Republicans felt that their leaders, and Bush, were ceding too much to the Democrats in the interest of harmony.

In the previous week, McCain had taken on another contentious issue: An amendment had been offered to remove from a bill authorizing funds for the Defense Department a provision creating a commission to recommend the closing of unneeded military bases. Senators with bases in their states objected, as usual, and in the last few years they had prevailed.

But this was an issue that went to McCain's disdain for pork, particularly when military funds would be wasted, particularly now. He was disturbed that even in a national crisis parochial interests might prevail. Speaking with some agitation on the Senate floor on Monday, McCain said, "The fact is, at a time when we rally around the President of the United States and the Secretary of Defense and the men and women in the armed services, we are going in direct contravention to the views of the President of the United States, the Secretary of Defense, and our military and civilian leadership. It is that clear."

He became a bit testy with his friend and usual ally, Susan Collins, who had just argued against more base closings (and who is up for reelection). "I would like for the Senator from Maine to talk to General Schwarzkopf. He is a fairly respected individual," he said somewhat snappishly. "I would like for her to hear all the former chairmen of the Joint Chiefs of Staff," he said. "It's business as usual in the United States Congress. We're not prepared to give up anything to fight this war on terrorism."

The next day, somewhat to his surprise, McCain's position on the base-closings prevailed, on a close vote.

·   ·   ·

On the Senate floor on Thursday morning, addressing the holdup of the airline safety bill, McCain said, "For us to delay because we have our own agenda here would be an abrogation of our responsibility."

McCain was frustrated because he believed that shoring up public confidence in flying was an urgent matter for the nation, psychologically and economically. And he was disturbed that Congress was getting back to business as usual so soon.

A meeting with Transportation Secretary Norman Mineta scheduled for Thursday afternoon was abruptly cancelled. McCain believed that the White House was about to agree to his position on federalizing baggage screeners, but then Mineta and other officials met with House Republican leaders and got a tongue-lashing.

The House Republican leaders—principally Majority Leader Armey and Whip DeLay—were unhappy that Bush had said at a breakfast meeting with the bipartisan congressional leaders that he would accept an airline safety bill that included federal screeners if that would expedite passage of the bill. The House Republican leaders made it clear at their meeting with Mineta that they wanted no expansion of the federal workforce and that they didn't want to be pushed around by the Senate. That McCain was sponsoring the bill might well have fed their resistance.

Armey and DeLay—Hastert was still trying to work with the Democrats—were already highly perturbed by the President's suggestion that he would consider additional spending in addition to tax cuts in the economic stimulus bill. The return to partisanship was now out in the open. "Neither party likes bipartisanship," a high administration official said to me.

At a Senate Republican conference meeting held that morning, George Voinovich, of Ohio, berated McCain and Kay Bailey Hutchinson, of Texas, a co-sponsor of the airline safety bill, saying that in a time of crisis the Republicans should agree to everything the administration wants. McCain stood up and said, "Then we should adjourn, because there's no reason for us to be here."

McCain said later that many Republicans "don't want more employees because that means more Democratic votes." This argument was actually made in the Republican conference that morning; the deeply held view of the right is that federal employees are ipso facto Democrats and therefore the size of the federal government should be reduced; it's a fundamental argument over power. The attacks on "big government" are in part philosophical, but they're also about Republican efforts to prevent the growth of the Democratic electorate. But it seemed unlikely that twenty-eight thousand people, scattered in airports throughout the land—representing 1.5 percent of the current federal work force (actually lower than it's been since 1960)—would tip the balance of power in the country.

McCain told the Republican conference, "We're going to federalize because the I.N.S. and other agencies for security and enforcement are federalized." (He was referring, of course, to the Immigration and Naturalization Service.)

Armey and DeLay wanted the stimulus program to be tax cuts only, including speeding up the recently passed tax bill's reduction in the top marginal rates and retroactive cuts for businesses—which would help the wealthiest and do little to stimulate the economy—as well as making the tax cuts permanent and cutting the capital gains tax. The White House had come out for a stimulus program that consisted mostly of speeding up the tax cuts for individuals and granting new breaks for businesses, with about one-fifth of it to help laid-off workers. House Democrats who had been working with the Republicans and the Bush administration on the economic plan accused Bush of caving in to the conservative Republican House leaders. Bush's action ripped the bipartisan facade that had been in place since September 11.

The Republicans on the House Ways and Means Committee soon thereafter rammed through their committee a tax bill that was highly generous to wealthy individuals and corporations and did little by way of stimulating the economy in the short term—and likely damaged it in the longer run—and in so doing undermined an understanding that Speaker Hastert had had with the Democrats that they should work out the economic program together. Once again, Hastert was trying to be reasonable but was undercut by his supposed lieutenants. And the fact that the nation was in a crisis did nothing to deter, or even embarrass, the special interests—from peanut growers to corporate lobbyists—from trying to capitalize on the situation.

Now, in his office, McCain takes a call from Josh Bolten, the White House Deputy Chief of Staff for Policy, to talk about the airline problem. In a friendly manner, McCain explains to Bolten his frustration over the issue. "We should be able to get it to the floor for debate," he says. "I'm too old to get angry, but I'm frustrated." After concluding the conversation, McCain tells Salter that he thinks Bolten "wants to work it out." He's clearly pleased with the thought that he can work with the White House on this issue and says, "They've got problems with them [the conservative House Republicans] not just with this; they have a problem on the stimulus."

On his way out of the office, McCain is quickly briefed by Sonya Sotak, who has been talking to Kennedy's staff and White House aides on a possible compromise on the patients' bill of rights. Like others on McCain's staff, Sotak knows how to deliver complicated information succinctly. McCain teases her about the state of her apartment, to which he and others had repaired just after the terrorist attacks on September 11.

McCain had hoped to go to New York that evening, to go to a baseball game with Giuliani. The David Letterman show had called and asked if McCain would be on the program that night—to be taped before the game. But McCain had regretted the two tempting invitations because of the possibility there would be a roll-call vote in the late afternoon. Then word comes that there will be no vote after all.

McCain says forlornly, "I could have gone to New York."

The following Wednesday, October 10, an obviously frustrated McCain, speaking on the Senate floor about the lack of action on the airline safety bill, says, "This is rapidly turning into a farce." In passing, he criticizes an anonymous administration official who recently told a congressional committee, relayed to the *Washington Post,* that there was a hundred percent chance of terrorist retaliation for the U.S.'s military action in Afghanistan, which had begun the previous Sunday. McCain believes that while Americans should be informed about the seriousness of the attacks on September 11, officials shouldn't be spreading fear. Then he returns to the airline safety bill.

"For nearly two weeks we have failed to have one moment of debate on this issue, and no amendment has been proposed. I find that, frankly, incomprehensible."

He continues, "I am not really renowned for my patience, but I believe I have shown a lot of patience." He says that the White House cancelled two meetings with him and Hollings in one day, something he had never seen before.

In his office that afternoon, McCain said, "The White House has been captured by the House leaders."

He added, "I'm not happy. I'm not angry. I'm not happy that we've got men and women putting themselves in harm's way for the good of this country and we cannot move on an airline security bill to give people more confidence and help the economy rebound."

That evening, after more negotiations on McCain's part—his heightened negotiating skills and his new standing in the Senate as a legislator were proving essential in the crisis—the Senate passed the airline safety bill 100–0. (The Democrats' proposal for aid to laid-off workers was put off.)

But the House Republican leaders had no intention of letting McCain's bill come to the House floor, so he was soon in his second great confrontation of the year with them. And the White House, at the urging of Tom DeLay, stiffened its resistance to federalizing the baggage screeners.

That weekend, McCain was to make another strenuous tour of his state.

Chapter 20

"I think you have to recognize that there is a reason for fear. . . . But you have to suppress it. You have to channel it."

WHILE MCCAIN was en route to Arizona, there was a new development in the nation's struggle against terrorism, which led to a new turn in his effort to reassure and guide the nation. Around noon on Friday, October 12, it was announced that an assistant to NBC News anchor Tom Brokaw had contracted anthrax, apparently from a letter addressed to Brokaw that she had opened. Until then, recent anthrax cases had been limited to American Media, a company based in Florida, which publishes tabloids; two people had been infected, and one had died. Several others had been exposed to the anthrax spores. Now a major news organization in New York City had been attacked, an event bound to rivet the attention of the public—and to spread panic.

As it happened, McCain had given an interview to columnist Walter Shapiro, of *USA Today*, on the subject of fear, and the column had appeared that morning. McCain, earlier in his life, in the North Vietnamese prison camps, had confronted fear. The column quoted McCain saying, "The way you live with fear is that you suppress it." He said, "Anyone who is faced with a life-threatening situation will have fear. Anyone who says they don't is either crazy or a liar. The trick is to channel it into productive missions and activities. That's the way I've handled it in the past."

McCain's comments in the *USA Today* column led to a request that he appear from Phoenix that night on Chris Matthews's *Hardball,* on CNBC, and invitations the following week to appear on *Good Morning America, Oprah,* the David Letterman show, *Imus in the Morning,* and *Meet the Press.* Some of the invitations followed the startling announcement on Tuesday, October 16, that anthrax had been found in the Hart Building office of Senate Majority Leader Tom Daschle and that numerous people had been exposed, a development that spawned more fear and panic. The anchors and the bookers of these shows knew whom to turn to. McCain's instinct for what the psyche of the nation needed was in perfect working order.

On Chris Matthews's show, McCain said, "I think you have to recognize that there is a reason for fear. . . . But you have to suppress it. You have to channel it, and it can be beneficial in a way because it will make you more alert. It'll make you more efficient. And it will make you more aware of everything that's going on around you. You know, Ernest Hemingway's famous definition of courage was 'grace under pressure.' And basically that's what he was saying. You've got to show grace under pressure and that grace is to go on with your life, not let it rule you, not let it overcome you."

On Wednesday afternoon, October 17, the U.S. Capitol, gleaming against an azure sky punctuated with leisurely snow-white clouds, looked like a picture on a calendar. Only when one got near did the hurt—real and psychological—that had been inflicted become apparent.

Huge cement planters had been placed in front of the steps of the Russell Building, presumably to prevent an attack by a truck going up the stairs. (Trucks had already been barred from the main roads on Capitol Hill.) The Capitol Plaza was blocked off to all traffic by placing cars across the roads to it.

That morning, panic had developed into near hysteria on Capitol Hill. There were rumors that sixty people in the Hart Office Building had been found to have been exposed to anthrax (at week's end the count was twenty-eight Senate staff members); that the anthrax spores from the letter sent to Daschle had spread into the ventilating systems and the tunnels of the Senate office buildings (the latter was untrue, the former not yet known); that the tunnels and subway leading from the Hart Building had been sealed off (also not true). Shortly before ten that morning, the House leadership, looking panicked, announced that they would go out of session that afternoon until the following Tuesday, during which time the House side of the Capitol and their offices would be swept. Hastert passed on as fact some of the misinformation going around Capitol Hill.

When they had met at the White House earlier that day to see the President off to China, the leaders of both chambers had discussed whether to close down (whether they had agreed to do so remained in dispute), but during a briefing later that morning of all senators in the Senate Dining Room on the anthrax situation, most of them rebelled at shutting down, saying that this would send the wrong signal. (They rarely meet on Fridays, anyway.) But the office buildings would be closed for sweeping and most of the staff would be sent home. Outraged House Republicans, who had expected the Senate to do as they had done, accused the Senate of acting symbolically—which was, of course, the point. Later, after traces of anthrax were found in a House annex, where mail is collected, and in two House members' offices, it was widely said that the criticism of the House for fleeing was unfair. But Hastert's panicky spreading of false rumors, and the House's failure of imagination on how to keep

159

going, or appear to keep going, as the Senate had done while its offices were swept, had done its damage to the national psyche.

The previous afternoon, McCain had called his staff into his office, to try to calm them. Standing behind the leather chair in front of his desk, McCain began by joking. "Because of everything that's happened," he said, "I've decided to put Joe Donohue in charge of any disaster." The staff laughed. The youthful Donohue is an office favorite. As in the camps, the scamp in McCain used humor to diffuse tension.

Then he grew serious, saying, "If anyone sees anything suspicious in the mail, report it to an authority, call the Capitol police." He continued, repeating what he'd said on television, "It's OK to be afraid, but we need to channel that fear and be aware of our surroundings."

He told his staff that the senators had been told in briefings that there's a separate emergency response team in the Capitol for anthrax, so they were in a safer place than others were.

"These are strange times," McCain acknowledged, and added, "I appreciate the hard work everyone's doing."

And he ended by joking again. Referring to Donohue, he said, "We're going to call him Commander. Joe, you can go over to my place and pick up a uniform."

Despite the fact that he had another appointment, McCain then went to the Dirksen Building, where his Commerce Committee staff have their offices (having been moved there after control of the Senate passed to the Democrats).

"Stop snoring. Get up," McCain said as he entered the staff's offices. Holding the back of Buse's chair, he joked along the same lines that he had with the other staff members. This time, referring to a tiny, dark-haired woman, McCain said, "I just want everyone to know Pia's going to be in charge." (Pia Pialorsi is the press secretary for the committee's minority.)

. . .

On Wednesday afternoon, in his office, McCain expresses his frustration that the House Republican leaders, in particular his old foe Tom DeLay, are holding up the Senate-passed airline safety bill and asking members to support the House leadership's alternative, which gives the President the flexibility to choose whether or not to federalize the baggage screeners.

Buse tells him that yesterday DeLay called in representatives of the airlines, which support McCain's bill, and reminded them of his help on the airline bailout bill.

After his staff leaves, McCain is asked if he thinks the House leaders panicked in deciding to shut the House down until Tuesday.

"I think Americans understand and feel very concerned about the situation. That was clearly the intent of the people who've done these things. Our job as leaders is to calm people down and not have people panic, or the terrorists succeed.

"Some people say we should shut down and go home. I say that would be raising the white flag. If we tell people to get on with their business and we go home, that sets a *fine* example."

What does he think about the F.B.I. having issued a warning on October 11 that there could be another terrorist attack over the "next several days"?

"I don't think that was the best way to present it, nor was the statement by the Attorney General that endorsed the leak that there was a hundred percent chance of retaliation if we used military force."

McCain then slathers sunscreen on his face—because of an episode last year of melanoma, successfully removed, he does this religiously when he's about to be exposed to the sun—in preparation for a press conference outdoors in which he's going to criticize the House Republican leaders for holding up the airline safety bill.

"We'll have some fun at this press conference," he says. Asked what he thinks of the tax cuts the House Ways and Means Committee has put in the stimulus package, McCain criticizes a couple of specific business breaks as "backpedaling." He says, "That has no stimulative effect, and their bill doesn't do anything about people who don't pay taxes. Payroll taxes should be reduced. The size [$100 billion] and the shape of the tax package makes no sense. The White House came out with the most duplicitous statement I've ever seen. Let me put it this way: they didn't support it but they support it." He jumps up to point out a story in that day's *Washington Post,* which states that White House spokesman Ari Fleischer said the White House backs the bill but it "included several items that the President did not propose."

As he prepares to leave for the press conference, McCain is asked when he foresees getting back to the campaign finance bill.

He expects work on it to begin again early in 2002, he says, and adds that he's talked to Gephardt about it and that's when Gephardt thinks he can go to members to get the remaining needed signatures. "There's still a compelling need for it," he says. "Look at what's going on with the stimulus bill. I foresee us sort of as a split personality. I believe the Congress will be supportive of the government in the war on terrorism and I believe you'll see business as usual on domestic issues.

"We're going to get back to the whole reform agenda. We still need to pursue it, whether there's war or peace."

McCain is planning to take a trip to Central Asia after the session ends, with Fred Thompson and Chuck Hagel; so he does compartmentalize, after all. (Some of McCain's traveling partners jokingly complain about the fact that he never stops in Paris or London.)

Nancy Ives has come in to spray his hair for the press conference (as a result of the torture in the camps, he can't raise his arms above his shoulders), and McCain squeals and makes funny noises as Ives sprays.

As McCain starts down the Russell Building corridor toward his car, Donohue pops out of one of the offices and points McCain in the opposite direction. (Donohue had taken McCain to and from a lunch downtown and dropped him off before putting the car through the security checks—mirrors run under the car, the trunk opened—that even a senator's car now undergoes before it can be parked on Capitol Hill.)

"Joe, you're demoted," McCain says in mock anger.

In McCain's car, Ives points him toward a street exit, the now narrowed approach to which is lined with barbed wire.

"You know, Nancy, you're sending us through Checkpoint Charlie, for Christ's sake," McCain complains in mock anger. Upon finding the exit blocked by a truck, McCain gives up, backs up the car, and says, "Let's just walk."

McCain swiftly moves across the Capitol Plaza to a stone patio across from the House side of the Capitol. Along the way, the few tourists who have ventured to Capitol Hill today whom he encounters call out their admiration for him and thank him for what he has been saying. At the press conference site, a sizeable number of reporters have gathered, as they usually do when McCain makes a press appearance.

"I just came from a briefing that was held for all senators where it was clear to me that every agency of government has been galvanized to protect members of Congress and their staffers," McCain says. "And yet we don't seem to feel that same sense of urgency as far as the airline passenger and traveling public is concerned. In fact, there appears to be a dramatic difference between the quick galvanization in response to a real emergency here on Capitol Hill, yet there doesn't seem to be any urgency amongst the House leadership to bring this bill forward. Why is that? One reason is because they don't have the votes." He says, "It's time to act. It's time to act," and he adds, "If something else happens there's going to be great responsibility on the part of those who failed to act."

After the press conference, a number of reporters still have questions for him.

One asks, "Do you think this is bordering on mass hysteria?"

"I think outside the Capitol, people are much more calm."

He's asked what he would say to the school children of America.

"I'd like to tell the students about the current crisis: Look. America is the greatest nation in the world, the strongest nation in the world. People have risen to the challenge. Finally, I say to the young people of America, be afraid. Don't be worried about being afraid. But don't let it incapacitate you."

As he races back to the Russell Building, a couple of people stop him for autographs. One asks him if he's concerned about the future of the war with terrorists.

"I think we'll have challenges in the future and we will overcome them as we have challenges in the past," he replies.

Continuing on, he notices that Pia Pialorsi is several feet in front of him.

"Pia! Pia!" McCain calls out. "I've demoted Joe and now you're in charge." Pialorsi laughs and keeps up her pace.

"Pia! I expect to see an operations manual on my desk tomorrow morning. A thick one."

Afterword

BY THE TIME the Congress adjourned for the year shortly before Christmas, the discharge petition to force the campaign finance bill back to the House floor was three signatures short, and reform backers were optimistic that they could obtain the rest soon after the Congress reconvened in January.

McCain's position on federalizing baggage screeners prevailed, but not before the President threw in with the House Republican leaders Dick Armey and Tom DeLay and prevailed in the House, but then had to back down in the face of public opinion. McCain also prevailed on the issues of Mexican trucks and base closings. He introduced his bill to provide more opportunities for young people to participate in national service and fought a provision in a farm bill that banned the importation of catfish not bred in the United States—to aid catfish growers in six southern states. (He gave a Senate speech on the subject of "When is a catfish other than a catfish?") He joined Senator Joe Lieberman in calling for an investigation into the intelligence failures that led to September 11.

But in the closing weeks of the session, his primary attention was on his abiding passion—reform—and he wove various issues before the Senate into that theme. He castigated lobbyists and members of Congress for their unembarrassed efforts to capitalize on the opportunities presented by legislation dealing with the aftermath of September 11, calling their actions "war profiteering." He criticized various examples of "pork" and stirred up press attention to a particularly flagrant boondoggle by which the Air Force was to lease a hundred new Boeing jets (which it hadn't requested), pay most of their cost, and give them back to Boeing to use.

"Sooner or later it's going to break," McCain said. "Americans are going to get fed up and rebel. They're going to demand reform because it's corruption. It's the worst I've ever seen. From Rick Shelby [Republican of Alabama] getting two million dollars more for a statue of Vulcan to Boeing, it's a total rip-off.

"They're without shame. I'm talking about members of Congress, not the lobbyists, who are doing what they're paid to do. It's the system that makes good people do bad things because of the corrupting influence of money. We've gone through cycles of corruption and reform before, and sooner or later we'll get to reform."

On January 24, 2002, the reform coalition obtained the final three signatures needed to force the campaign finance bill to the House floor. It was widely believed that the ballooning Enron scandal had made the difference, but while it may well have sped up the process of getting the signatures, they most likely would have become available at some point anyway.

The foes of reform decided on the strategy of arguing that the bill didn't go far enough—that soft money should be eliminated altogether—while the Shays-Meehan bill permitted limited donations of soft money to state party entities. The evident purpose was to try to split the reform coalition, some of whom opposed any soft money and some of whom were demanding it. At the same time, the opponents were still also backing the Ney bill, which allowed quite a lot of soft money to remain in the system. The inconsistency didn't seem to bother them.

On the morning of February 13, when the House was to take up the bill, McCain warned in a press conference against adopting amendments that might force it to a conference between the House and the Senate. He also appeared on three morning television programs to push his message.

The reform forces easily won early roll-call votes, rejecting Republican proposals to ban all soft money. But the reformers ran into trouble when the Republicans stirred up a storm over a provision that they charged allowed the Democrats to borrow hard money before the next election and pay it back afterward with soft money; the goal was to drive Republican reformers away from the bill. The provision didn't actually say that, but it was ambiguous enough to exploit.

The issue was further muddied by the fact that Democratic National Committee Chairman Terence McAuliffe sought, and received, a special exemption in the bill to spend soft money after the election for the construction of a new party headquarters.

Republicans who were badly needed for passage of the bill began to get nervous. Some threatened to vote for an amendment sponsored by the Republican leadership to make the effective date of the new law immediate—cutting off any ability to raise soft money after that.

The Democrats, fearing that they would be at a disadvantage in hard money in the upcoming election, had decided—despite McCain's misgivings—to make the effective date of the new law November 6, the day after the 2002 elections, rather than the original bill's thirty days after enactment.

McCain, in his office that afternoon, was grim. Quietly perturbed, he made calls to House Republicans; he doesn't yell or carry on during such a crisis, in this case one that threatened years of effort on his part. He asked the trusted and steady Mike Castle, Republican of Delaware, to whip the moderate Republicans. McCain said to his advisers, "They never should have put in vague language like that. It's aggravating because everything was on track. Now we have a huge crisis here. All this happened because of their goddamn building."

Afterword

. . .

After some Republican reformers, and Gephardt, asked him to come over to the House side to help, McCain, who had been both eager and hesitant all afternoon—remembering the ruckus he'd caused when he'd gone over to the House last summer—went in the late afternoon with Salter to the House side where they parked themselves in room H 151. McCain met with usually pro-reform Republicans who were now shaky, ticking off their names on a list he and Salter carried.

Meanwhile, the coalition of Democrats and moderate Republicans behind the bill successfully fended off Republican leadership amendments designed to splinter the coalition by tempting away Blacks, gun supporters, veterans, and others by exempting them from the restrictions on ads. Gephardt, whose reform credentials were not so long ago in doubt, was regularly delivering two hundred or more votes for the bill.

Behind the scenes, reform lawyers drafted wording to deal with the hard/soft money problem, which McCain insisted on making more specific, and the change was easily adopted by the House. (The exception for Terry McAuliffe's building was knocked out on a roll-call vote.) Hard-money contributions were raised to two thousand dollars.

The Republicans' proposal to make the new law effective immediately was unworkable and probably unconstitutional (creating retroactive crimes), and it was resoundingly defeated. At 2:48 A.M. the House passed the bill by a comfortable vote of 240–189. Forty-one Republicans voted for it, eight of them freshmen, who had withstood terrific pressure from the leadership.

Thus another large step was taken toward the Congress's finally passing a significant campaign finance reform bill. It remained only for the Senate to approve the House-passed bill, fulfilling the pre-conference strategy the reformers had envisioned for over a year.

The next morning, McCain was alone in his office, standing by his desk, reading the *Washington Post* sports page.

He began to feel better about the way things were going, he said, when the amendment to exempt the NRA from the curbs on electioneering ads was defeated (in the closest vote of the night). "They pulled out all the stops on that.

"We were pretty confident—you never get confident, you're hopeful.

"You just keep a tight emotional rein. I don't feel any sense of relief or happiness until it's done." And then he talked about his effort to hold his emotions in check, which he'd talked about throughout this fight, in a new way.

"I learned from prison, you don't go too far high because then you go down."

He explained, "While I was in prison, in 1968 LBJ stopped bombing in North Vietnam, and a peace conference was convened in Paris. All of us—*all of us*—were very high. The ensuing months and years taught us otherwise. Never get too happy or too depressed. I try to maintain a tight rein on my emotions when in difficulty ever since."

Despite the fact that the House has passed a bill quite similar to that passed by the Senate, and that the majority of the Senate was willing to accept it and send it to the President, and that McCain now appeared to have enough votes to break a filibuster, Mitch McConnell wasn't done. Both sides worked on the votes on a possible filibuster: McConnell picked off one supporter of the bill, McCain picked off three who had voted against it but said they wouldn't support a filibuster, but the votes of three other Republicans who had supported the bill were in some doubt. Reformers worried that McConnell was trying to buy time to persuade them.

McConnell said he had just a few "technical" amendments to offer, but any change in the bill would once again threaten a conference. And some of his proposals were far from technical. McCain, trying to appear reasonable, met with McConnell several times in the office of Chuck Hagel and offered McConnell a separate bill containing technical changes he could accept. McConnell could offer his substantive amendments to the bill itself, but he and McCain knew that a majority would vote against changing it. McConnell wouldn't buy, and McCain wouldn't budge.

Gradually, the opposing side collapsed. McConnell, seeing that he didn't have the votes, said that he wouldn't filibuster. Trent Lott, figuring the Republicans had nothing to gain from holding up the bill any longer, was openly stating that he didn't favor a filibuster. Such had been the change in climate over the past year. But Phil Gramm was still threatening to filibuster. Daschle countered by saying this time they'd have to conduct a real filibuster—and, for emphasis, had cots produced—and not get away with simply a threat. He also vowed to have the Senate pass the bill by March 22, the Friday before the Easter recess.

Gramm gave up as well, and Republicans decided to get the thing over with. And so, in the early afternoon of Wednesday, March 20, the Senate voted by an overwhelming 68–32 to cut off any filibuster; three hours later it adopted the House-passed bill by a vote of 60–40 and sent it to the President, who said he would sign it. McCain, whom the White House viewed as a nuisance at best, had left him no choice. (McConnell's technical amendments were passed later.) True to his nature, McCain's reaction to the culmination of his years of effort was subdued, and also he wished not to gloat. "I'm happy, I'm happy," he insisted to reporters.

Something of enormous, historic significance had happened. After many long years of stalemate and frustration, the Congress had approved legislation to remove the most egregious, corrupting element of the campaign-finance system. It wasn't a perfect bill, as McCain kept saying, and of course people would try to find ways around it, as they do with any regulatory law. Most of the so-called unintended consequences predicted by critics had been considered by the bill's backers, but they thought the possible tradeoffs worth it. Other problems in the campaign finance system remained to be addressed. But something had taken place in both the Senate and the House that, a little over a year before, few had thought possible. A number of people, working together in unusual synchrony on Capitol Hill, helped it happen. But one man, through his determination, guts, steadiness, political acumen, and feel for the American people's better nature made it happen.

Early on Wednesday morning, March 27, surrounded by the Vice President and a few staff members, the President signed the campaign finance bill into law, thus avoiding a public ceremony at which its sponsors would be present. From Phoenix, John McCain issued a one-sentence statement: "I'm pleased that President Bush has signed campaign finance reform into law."

Acknowledgments

THERE ARE A NUMBER of people without whose help this book would not have been possible. In the office of Senator John McCain, Mark Salter, his chief of staff, and Nancy Ives, his director of communications, made sure to find ample time for me in their busy boss's schedule, and filled in the background on matters that came up as well as helped me understand McCain's thinking on certain issues. Mark Buse, his chief legislative strategist, could explain the most complicated maneuvers and make it fun. McCain himself was enormously patient with me—especially when I persisted in trying to know the various levels on which he functioned and thought—as well as extremely generous with his time. Although this book was written with the cooperation of the McCain office, it is in no sense an authorized book; neither he nor his staff will know what's in it until it's published. No one sat in on my interviews with McCain.

Others on McCain's staff who are owed thanks for their help are Rebecca Hanks, Ellen Cahill, and Joe Donohue. Other sources who helped—many are named in this book—have my gratitude.

Alice Mayhew, my editor at Simon & Schuster, brought to this project vision, her exceptional enthusiasm and energy, and smart editorial judgment. Having Alice Mayhew as your editor is having the wind at your back. Others at Simon & Schuster who helped see the book on its way are Anja Schmidt, Jonathan Jao, Gypsy da Silva, Gabriel Weiss, Victoria Meyer, and Elizabeth Hayes. My agent, Andrew Wylie, energetically saw to it that this book was published. Many friends gave me moral support; those who did that as well as actually help on the book itself, and deserve thanks, are Jim Jaffe, Sudie Nolan, Francis O'Brien, and Leslie Sewell. And then there is my husband and total partner, David Webster, whose support and wise judgment have been integral to this as well as everything that I do.

Index

Index

Bush administration (*cont.*)
  energy legislation of, 123
  final campaign finance bill and, 170
  first state dinner of, 129, 130
  Hagel bill and, 7, 24, 25, 26, 54, 86
  McCain-Feingold bill and, 6–7,
    9–10, 14, 15–17, 24, 31, 59, 72
  and McCain's possible presidential
    bid, 76
  McCain's relationship with, 14,
    15–16, 71, 72, 76–77, 78, 84,
    113, 123, 128, 130, 135, 136,
    146, 170
  McCain supporters shunned by, 77,
    123
  patients' bill of rights and, 72, 117,
    122–23, 124
  Shays-Meehan bill and, 86
  tax bill and, 71, 73–74, 78, 79, 103,
    137
Bush v. Gore, 60, 62

campaign finance reform:
  in election of 2000, 1, 3–5, 69–70
  final passage of, 166–70
  House and, *see* Shays-Meehan bill
  McCain on, 1, 3, 4, 15, 24, 47,
    166–67
  Senate and, *see* McCain-Feingold bill
  Theodore Roosevelt and, 12, 91
campaign finance system, problems of,
  3, 4, 15, 24, 34, 104, 166–67
Campaign for America, 112, 118, 143
Capitol, 139
  anti-terrorism measures at, 158–59,
    163
  September 11th terrorist attacks and,
    131, 132, 147
Capitol Hill Club, 97
Castle, Mike, 167
catfish, importation of, 165
CBS, 134, 137
Center for Conservative Reform, 79–80
Charlie Rose Show, The, 139
Cheney, Dick, 2, 16, 17, 18, 54, 63, 149
Christian right, 60, 62
Clinton, Bill, 19, 45, 96
Clinton, Hillary, 13
Clinton administration, 13, 78, 134,
  136

CNBC, 138, 158
CNN, 44, 138, 139, 141, 145
Cochran, Thad, 10–11, 53, 54
college sports, gambling and, 71–72
Collins, Susan, 10, 15, 44, 45, 151
Committee for Economic
    Development, 19, 112
Common Cause, 19, 52, 62, 93, 112,
    118
Condit, Gary, 91
Congress, U.S.:
  post-September 11th bipartisanship
    in, 144, 150–51, 152–54, 162
  September 20th Bush address to, 146
Conrad, Kent, 137
Conservative Action Team, 95
Consumer Products Safety
    Commission, 114, 125
corporations:
  paycheck protection and, 40–41
  soft money and, 4, 12, 16, 49
Corzine, Jon, 27–28

Daschle, Linda, 74
Daschle, Tom:
  anthrax threat and, 158, 159
  final passage of bill and, 170
  McCain-Feingold bill and, 3, 24, 26,
    36, 44, 45, 46, 50, 52, 55, 56, 58,
    60, 82, 99, 109, 110
  as McCain's ranch guest, 74–75, 76,
    79
  Shays-Meehan bill and, 82, 87, 92, 99
Davis, Rick, 52, 79, 118, 126
Davis, Tom, 5
Defense Department, U.S., 151
DeLay, Tom, 17
  airline safety bill and, 152, 156, 161,
    165
  economic stimulus bill and, 152, 153
  Shays-Meehan bill and, 59, 81,
    85–86, 90, 95, 98, 100, 101,
    105
Democracy 21, 93, 112
Democratic Congressional Campaign
    Committee, 117–18
Democratic National Committee, 30,
    167
Democratic Senatorial Campaign
    Committee, 63

Index

Index

Index

Index

Index

Index

Index

About the Author

ELIZABETH DREW is the much-honored author of eleven previous books about national politics, including *The Corruption of American Politics, Whatever It Takes, Showdown,* and *On the Edge.* A distinguished television and radio commentator, Elizabeth Drew lives in Washington, D.C.